ONE HUNDRED YEARS OF CHILDHOOD

One Hundred Years of
Childhood

compiled and edited by
RICHARD EDWARDS

One Hundred Years of Childhood
Richard Edwards

Published by Aspect Design 2012
Malvern, Worcestershire, United Kingdom.

Designed and Printed by Aspect Design
89 Newtown Road, Malvern, Worcs. WR14 1PD
United Kingdom
Tel: 01684 561567
E-mail: books@aspect-design.net
Website: www.aspect-design.net

All Rights Reserved.

Copyright © 2012 Richard Edwards
Except pp.103–114 Copyright © 2012 P J Fallon

Richard Edwards has asserted his moral right
to be identified as the author of this work.

The right of Richard Edwards to be identified as the author
of this work has been asserted in accordance with
Section 77 of the Copyright, Designs and Patents Act 1988.

This book is sold subject to the condition that it shall not, by way of trade or otherwise, be lent, resold, hired out or otherwise circulated without the publisher's prior consent in any form of binding or cover other than that in which it is published and without a similar condition including this condition being imposed on the subsequent purchaser.

A copy of this book has been deposited with the British Library Board.

Cover Design Copyright © 2012 Aspect Design.
Original photograph Copyright © 2012 Nik Silver

ISBN 978-1-908832-07-8

*For Isabelle, Julian, Maisie, Sanjay and Megan.
Children and citizens of the twenty-first century.*

CONTENTS

Introduction 9
Timeline of British Social History: 1900–1924 19
James Edwards 27
Joan Edwards 33
Arwyn Jones 38
Ivan Geffen 41
Ted Barton 51
Timeline of British Social History: 1925–1950 57
Maureen Wildash 66
Jean Richardson 71
Gill Holt 80
Gren Gaskell 85
Easton Wren 91
Elisabeth Donnelly 96
Patrick Fallon 103
Robin Ellis 115
Barry Wills 118
John Jansen 132
Timeline of British Social History: 1951–1975 137
Stephen Lay 148

Carol Lay	155
Barry Austin	161
Lucy Conrad	167
Rebecca Edwards	172
Timeline of British Social History: 1976–1999	178
Peter Cousins	187
Catherine Pitt	192
Acknowledgements	198
Bibliography	199

INTRODUCTION

The seeds of this project were sown many years ago when I asked my parents to write accounts of their early twentieth century childhoods. They both responded and their memories were duly passed around the family and then stored away in a dusty filing cabinet. Recently it occurred to me that their memories represented an interesting aspect of social history so I decided to try and extend these narratives across the twentieth century. The immediate problem was in deciding who would fill the gap, but after a few false starts I resorted to the family telephone book! As a result the twenty-two contributions which form the core of this book are made up largely by my friends and family. This approach immediately raises fears about how representative the accounts are. Do they merely represent the musings of a privileged white middle class sector of society? It will become clear from reading the narratives that follow that my contributors come from a range of social and geographical backgrounds, although the bias is certainly white and English. Nine of the authors grew up in working class families whereas the remainder had childhoods set in the middle class, some more privileged than others. The places recorded in these memoirs range from Sennen, on the distant shore of West Cornwall, to Ayrshire in Scotland and include isolated rural communities, small villages, towns of varying size and the cities of London, and Liverpool.

I have grouped the contributions into four equal periods of the twentieth century together with a timeline, which provides the political and socio-economic context in which families lived out their lives.

Children do not grow up in a vacuum and are as much influenced by events and changes in society as adults. The period from 1900–1924 spanned the Great War and defines a period when cars were few and far between and screens were confined to the cinema. My parents, James and Joan Edwards, whose accounts initiated this project, died some years ago. However, the three additional authors writing about this period are still alive and writing-fit if not fighting-fit. Their accounts tell of a world which has largely vanished.

The period from 1925–1950 was characterised by mass unemployment and dominated by the Second World War and the harsh economic conditions which followed. Ten of the authors are from this period and their accounts clearly vary according whether they were living in urban or rural areas. Thus Easton Wren was clearly traumatised by the nightly bombing raids in Ayrshire whereas Gill Holt's childhood in Oxfordshire was largely idyllic. One aspect which affected many children in the 1940s was the return of fathers after a long absence in the forces and this is touched on briefly by Easton Wren. My own early years were spent in a very comfortable nest presided over by my mother and grandmother. This agreeable existence was sharply disrupted by my father's return from military service in North Africa. Suddenly a much harsher regime was introduced and my father's frequent moods of sullen anger perceptibly lowered the temperature within the home.

The five contributors who were born in the period from 1951–1975 were the beneficiaries of an increasingly affluent society although the childhoods described here reflect much of the simplicity of earlier times. But by now television had become a dominant influence in all of our lives.

The period from 1976–1999 sees the advent of computers, the internet and mobile phones. However, the accounts by Peter Cousins and Catherine Pitt suggest that these inventions only touched lightly on their lives. Sadly I was unable to obtain more accounts from this period in spite of many requests.

One of the questions which has loomed increasingly large as the project developed is whether the nature of childhood has changed during the twentieth century. My belief is that it started to change in the final decades in fundamental ways and so in many ways this book

INTRODUCTION

is about a childhood experience which has largely disappeared. This is an aspect I will return to later.

I consider that these childhood memories, ranging across some ninety years, will largely speak for themselves but I cannot resist searching for some common threads and highlighting some significant changes. The most consistent aspect of twentieth century childhood was the total freedom and 'out of doors' environment which seems to be reflected in nearly all the narratives presented here. Two further aspects I wish to examine are the nature of discipline and the impact of technological change.

The context of my own childhood in the 1940s and 1950s was an up-market estate at the very margins of the Merseyside conurbation, whose outward expansion had been brought to an abrupt halt, frozen by the outbreak of the Second World War. A group of children of similar age from the estate formed an informal gang whose members fluctuated over the years, but with a core membership which lasted throughout my school days. Our home lay at the end of a cul-de-sac, beyond which extended fields, woods and ponds, which became my every day environment. The pond, some yards away from the house, was a particular attraction. Here frogspawn was collected annually but rarely grew into fully-fledged frogs. Planks and logs became ocean liners and were floated from side to side. In the winter we rejoiced in the snow and ice and made our own judgement about whether it was safe to slide on the surface of the pond, nobody fell through the ice. Sledging was a favourite winter sport. I can still remember the joy when my brother and I were given a sledge by my parents one Christmas. Thundering down a sleep slope on a sledge was probably the highlight of my childhood, and adults were nowhere to be seen.

One summer holiday my elder brother, John, inspired no doubt by films of escaping prisoners of war, supervised the construction of a tunnel which extended for some distance into a bank adjacent to the pond! An additional playground was the barn belonging to the local farmer, Mr Pimbley, who must have been a saintly man. We built elaborate dens amongst the bales of straw and swung on ropes from the rafters. Occasionally pavements and roads became the playground as cars were few and far between: roller skating, cricket, and 'kingy'

The Poulton Hey estate gang (circa 1951).
I am in the front row (centre) and my brother, John, in the back row (left)

(described by Robin Ellis) were my favourite pastimes. Parents played no part in these activities and they were only vaguely aware of our whereabouts. We simply disappeared after breakfast and re-appeared when we became hungry. Nearly all the contributors echo this experience in varying degrees.

Another common factor which enhanced the pleasure of the 'out-of-doors' environment was the bicycle. I was amused to note that James Edwards and Peter Cousins, writing from different ends of the century, both recalled a cycling mishap. For many of my generation a new bike was the reward for passing the dreaded eleven plus examination, the preparation for which dominated the last year of primary school. I passed the exam, to my parents' pleasure and surprise and my treasured possession was a Raleigh Lenton with drop handle bars, boasting the signature of Reg Harris on the cross bar. Unfortunately my father, a natural Luddite, was totally opposed to gears of any description. This presented few problems in the gently undulating landscape of the Wirral peninsula but was a serious drawback on journeys into North Wales. In any event the bicycle extended our world far beyond the

INTRODUCTION

On yer bikes! I am in the foreground with friends
David and Marie Dala outside our homes in Bebington.

immediate neighbourhood and was also our means of travelling to school, come rain or shine. If twentieth century childhood required an iconic symbol it would probably be a bicycle.

Discipline, often in the form of physical punishment, was something that you expected as a child for much of the twentieth century and 'spare the rod and spoil the child' might have been written as a strap line. However, the accounts written by those growing up in the sixties and later decades suggest a more benign approach to discipline had begun. For those growing up in the first half of the century physical violence could be meted out at home, as mentioned by Gren Gaskell, or at school. I was quite shocked to read about the corporal punishment regularly inflicted on primary school children which is recorded by Robin Ellis, Gill Holt and John Jansen and the daily violence described by Patrick Fallon at St Mary's College is appalling.

Punishment was not confined to home or school. Any adult felt able to administer a smack if they felt it was appropriate. I remember a winter's afternoon, when snow covered the ground when I was returning home from school and relishing the experience. At one point I daringly threw a speculative snowball across the road towards a group of workmen and to my surprise and horror it hit one of them smack between the shoulders. The man ran towards me as I stood transfixed, like a rabbit in car headlights. He then proceeded to give me a good hiding. I did not mention this on my return home as my mother would not have expected anything else. In fact on several occasions I saw her hit children who she thought were out of order. In retrospect these punishments seem outrageous but for much of the time children accepted it as normal and certainly knew when they had crossed a boundary.

Evolving technologies clearly had a major influence on childhood. Perhaps the dominant development was the rise in the number of cars. This may have widened the scope for family holidays, as recalled by Carol Lay, but increasingly denied children the street as a place to play which is recalled by Ted Barton and Barry Wills.

The technologies associated with communication have had a massive impact on childhood although not highlighted by any of my authors. During my early years at primary school I was issued with an old piece of slate and some chalk, but eventually graduated to paper and a scratchy pen, dipped into ink wells which seemed to contain as much solids as ink. At Grammar school we aspired to fountain pens and large bottles of ink of varying hues. Many years later I wrote a text book using a biro and copious quantities of Tippex. I nervously decided to take the plunge into using a PC in the mid 1990s but I am happily typing this manuscript with an Apple Mac. Where will it end?

Technology has also transformed our entertainment during the twentieth century. Consider the life of Arwyn Jones. Arwyn went to bed by candlelight and strained alongside his brothers to hear the voices cracking from a crystal radio set. Today he listens to classical music on his MP3, e-mails his friends and flies regularly to the USA to visit his daughter. What changes in one lifetime!

The introduction of radio and television were key landmarks in the experience of twentieth century children. In my own case radio was paramount. *Children's Hour* was a must but I also enjoyed *Toy Town, Dick Barton, Journey into Space* and *The Goon Show*. My father disliked popular music of any kind and it was virtually banned from the home.

One consequence of this censorship was that during the late 1940s the tune 'Open the Door, Richard' was very popular on the radio and nearly every adult greeted me with this catch phrase. But I did not hear the tune myself until 2011, when I listened to it on *YouTube*. However, as a teenager I discovered that the stations for Radio Luxembourg and the Third Programme were only millimetres apart so that as soon as I heard my father's key turning in the lock of the front door the programme was changed in an instant, so Frankie Vaughan became Vaughan Williams at the touch of a dial. Television dramatically changed the situation from a listening and imaginative experience to more passive viewing, but the pleasures of favourite programmes are recalled with fondness by Rebecca Edwards and Lucy Conrad.

One aspect of childhood which none of my contributors have mentioned was the rhythms which characterised the year although many have highlighted the joy of the summer holidays, but there were cyclical events which marked the passing of the year. Some of these were dictated by the seasons, so that the autumn months were devoted to conkers. A hardy conker might survive up to twenty bouts and I favoured the 'cheese cutter' shape. Unscrupulous fellow pupils would soak their conkers in vinegar so that they became hard, green shrivelled objects so these processed creations always prevailed in the end. Another highlight of the year was Bonfire Night on 5 November when my brother and I would sally forth with our pockets bulging with fireworks, principally bangers and rip-raps, but I gained as much pleasure in the construction of the bonfire, a ritual which lasted for some weeks. Living near woods and fields meant that there was always a plentiful supply of material to be collected and the resulting structure was enormous. The final pleasure was roasting potatoes in the dying embers. Personally Bonfire Night and its associated pleasures surpassed the Christmas festivities. The year was also punctuated by games such as marbles, which I loved and five-stones where I lacked the necessary expertise. I never worked out who knew when the new phase would begin or end. It just happened and I joyfully embraced the new craze.

My timeline of the twentieth century highlights what I believe have been the principal events and discoveries which have affected the lives of ordinary people. For example, my father James Edwards was born in the same year that Orville and Wright flew for the first time but his own experience of flight was mainly restricted to being flown home from Algeria on compassionate leave in 1942 when I was critically ill with measles and pneumonia. I believe that the technology associated with mechanised warfare had a more profound effect on his childhood with the death of his elder brother, John, at the Somme and with many young people leaving his home town of Wallasey to be slaughtered on the battle fields of northern France. Probably the gramophone was the only twentieth century invention of which my father approved. In contrast my mother, Joan Edwards, embraced all new technology and her fascination with cars was surpassed only by her love of dogs and cats.

My own arrival in the world coincided with the evacuation of Allied troops from Dunkirk which was probably one of the most pivotal weeks in the history of the twentieth century. Needless to say I was unaware of the historic nature of my timing but in later years asked my mother if she had been worried by giving birth in such terrible times 'Oh no! There wasn't much happening at that time,' was her amazing response. Had she been preoccupied with domestic matters or merely forgotten? I shall never know.

Now I would like to turn to the question of whether the childhood experience in this country has changed significantly in recent decades. I firmly believe that it has. Nearly all the twenty-two accounts in the following pages suggest a happy childhood, with the chilling exception of Gren Gaskell, in spite of the harsh discipline that many experienced. However, there are strong indications that childhood in this country is no longer a happy experience. A comprehensive study of children in twenty-one OECD countries was carried out during the early years of this century by UNHCR. The results make startling reading and show that children growing up in the UK are the least happy of all the countries surveyed. The well-being of children was assessed using six parameters which are listed below with the position of the UK indicated in brackets:

>Material well-being (eighteenth).
>Health and Safety (twelfth).
>Educational well-being (seventeenth).

> Family and peer relations (twenty-first).
> Behaviour and risks (twenty-first).
> Subjective well-being (twenty-first).

Let us take just one of these factors, family and peer relationships, for closer examination. The score for each country was based on averaging separate scores for family structure, extent of interaction with parents, and peer relationships in which eleven, thirteen and fifteen-year-olds were asked if their peers were 'kind and helpful'. The UK came at or near the bottom on each parameter. Clearly we do not have the data from earlier years for comparison but the breakdown of conventional family life can be measured. For example, in 1950 there were 408,000 marriages and 33,000 divorces compared with 1990 when there were 375,000 marriages and 168,000 divorces.

The poor sense of well-being of children in the UK must result from a combination of factors relating to both family life and relationships with friends. Family relationships are adversely affected by the high rate of divorce and the pressures on parents having to work. Mass marketing aimed at children must surely affect their attitudes and aspirations. For example, clothing with the correct brand has become a badge of merit and bullying may be related to not having the correct gear. Not being 'cool' marks you as an outsider.

Increasingly, childhood in the later years of the twentieth century became a supervised indoor experience. Again several factors have to be taken into account. The large number of cars on the road is perceived as a threat. For much of the century children walked or cycled to school but nowadays they are much more likely to be delivered and collected. High-profile cases of child abduction give parents a sense of anxiety about the safety of their loved ones. The advent of television and computers means that 'playing outside' has been increasingly replaced by a screen-based childhood. A recent study by researchers at Loughborough and Bristol Universities (*Guardian,* 3 August, 2011) questioned ten and eleven-year-olds and found children often had access to five different devices at any one time. The researchers suggested that the sedentary life styles were linked to obesity and mental health problems.

An additional factor is the culture of Health and Safety, which in turn is driven by greedy lawyers. Recently my eight-year old grandson wrote out a list of activities which were prohibited at his primary school as a consequence of Health and Safety regulations. The list included playing conkers or marbles, athletics, cricket, baseball, football with a hard ball and roller skating. This summary includes many of the activities which made my own childhood so happy. Risk aversion intended to remove all possibility of an accident has hugely diminished the pleasures of childhood, and children know it.

My book is a record of childhood through the twentieth century based on the experiences of twenty-two individuals from differing parts of the country and from differing social backgrounds. Nearly all of them have looked back on their childhood as a happy stage of their lives. For many it was a sort of paradise. Have we lost the paradise of childhood and what are we doing about it?

TIMELINE OF BRITISH SOCIAL HISTORY: 1900–1924

1900

General Election won by the Conservatives with Lord Salisbury as PM.
The Labour Party created with Keir Hardie as its leader.
Average family size: 3.5 children.
Infant mortality rate was 140 deaths per 1,000 births (7 deaths per 1,000 in 1990).
Edward Elgar's *Dream of Gerontius* premiered in Birmingham.
Daily Express founded.
Popular published songs included 'Absence Makes the Heart Grow Fonder' and 'A Bird in a Gilded Cage'.

1901

Death of Queen Victoria and accession of King Edward VII.
UK population reached 38.3 million: 15% of the population over the age of 50.
Marconi conducted the first successful transatlantic experimental radio communication.
Life expectancy for new-born boys was 45 years and 49 years for girls (73.8 years and 79.1 years in 1992).
Frank Hornby took out a patent for 'Meccano'.

1902

Second Boer War ended.
Education Act passed by the Balfour Government, which created Local

Education Authorities and laid the foundations for a national system of secondary education.

Birth of the 'Teddy Bear'.

Factory producing 'Marmite' opened in Burton-on-Trent.

Ransomes produced the first commercially available petrol-driven lawn mower.

E Nesbit published *Five Children and It* and Beatrix Potter published *The Tale of Peter Rabbit*.

1903

Orville and Wilbur Wright made the first powered, sustained and controlled flight in a heavier-than-air machine.

German company AEG tested an electric locomotive with a speed of 130.5 miles per hour.

Emmeline Pankhurst founded the Women's Social and Political Union at a meeting in London, which became the suffragette movement.

Daily Mirror founded.

Edward Binney and Harold Smith co-invented crayons.

Publication of *The Call of the Wild* by Jack London.

1904

Entente Cordiale signed between Britain and France.

In the USA Henry Ford set a new land speed record of 91.37 miles per hour. In Britain the speed limit on roads was 20 miles per hour. Car number plates introduced.

Britain's first surface electric trains ran between Liverpool and Southport.

The celebration of Empire Day introduced.

Thomas Sullivan invented the tea bag.

First production of J M Barrie's play *Peter Pan*.

1905

First public protest by suffragettes led by Emmeline Pankhurst at Westminster.

HMS *Dreadnought* laid down, revolutionising battleship design and triggering a naval arms race.

GPO London to Brighton horse-drawn parcel post carriage replaced by a lorry.

'Aspirin' sold in the UK for the first time.

Dr Thomas Barnardo died. The charity he founded ran 96 homes caring for 8,500 children.

H G Wells published *Kipps* and E M Forster published *Where Angels Fear to Tread*.

1906

General Election won by the Liberal Party under Henry Campbell-Bannerman.

10% of women in paid work (of whom 33% were in domestic service).

The world's largest ship, RMS *Lusitania*, launched in Glasgow.

The first German submarine entered the German Imperial Navy.

William Kellogg invented 'Cornflakes'.

Publication of *The Railway Children* by E Nesbit and *White Fang* by Jack London.

1907

Horatio Phillips achieved the first limited, powered, heavier-than-air flight over a distance of 500 feet.

Colour photography invented by August and Louis Lumière.

Baden Powell held an experimental camp on Brownsea Island, Dorset, to test out his ideas about the Scout movement.

A system of free places in grammar schools initiated.

James Spangler invented a portable electric vacuum cleaner.

1908

First publication of *The Magnet*, a boys' weekly paper which featured the character Billy Bunter 'the Fat Owl of the Remove'.

Publication of *Scouting for Boys*.

The Sanderson Tractor and Implement Co of Bedford introduced a four-wheel, petrol-driven tractor and became the largest tractor manufacturer outside the USA.

Pathé invented the newsreel, which was shown in cinemas before the film.

Publication of *Anne of Green Gables* by Lucy Maud Montgomery and

Wind in the Willows by Kenneth Grahame.

1909

Louis Bleriot made the first crossing of the English Channel in an aeroplane.

The first purpose-built cinemas in UK were constructed.

Invention of instant coffee by G Washington.

Girl Guides movement founded.

1910

Death of King Edwards VII and accession to the throne of George V.

Two General Elections, both won by the Liberal Party under Herbert Asquith.

Thomas Eddison demonstrated the first talking motion picture.

Gracie Fields first appeared in variety in Rochdale.

Publication of *Mr Polly* by H G Wells.

1911

Coronation of King George V who was also crowned Emperor of India in New Delhi.

UK population reached 42·1 million. 63% of people died before the age of 60.

14% of employed people were domestic servants.

The Official Secrets Act was passed and MPs voted to receive salaries.

Ernest Rutherford formulated his model of the atom with a small positively charged nucleus orbited by electrons. He is regarded as the father of nuclear physics.

2,000 cinemas open in the UK.

Frances Hodgson Burnett published *The Secret Garden*.

1912

Royal Flying Corps (RFC) established, precursor of RAF.

The National Insurance Act came into force, introducing National Insurance payments.

The RMS *Titanic* sank on its maiden voyage, resulting in the death of 1517 people.

Infectious diseases prevalent among children and were a significant factor in infant mortality, accounting for 50% of child deaths.

Suffragette movement adopted militant tactics.

1913

Suffragette Emily Davison died after falling under the King's horse at the Epsom Derby.

UK coal production peaked at 287 million tons.

Morris Motor Company opened a factory at Cowley, Oxford.

D H Lawrence published *Sons and Lovers*.

Crossword puzzle invented by Arthur Wynne.

1914

Outbreak of First World War.

Hostilities included the First Battle of the Marne in which two million Allied troops took part (263,000 killed or wounded).

Britain's first aircraft carrier, HMS *Ark Royal*, commissioned.

Britain bombed for the first time, in Dover.

The rate of owner occupation in UK was 10%.

24% of women in full-time employment.

Bernard Shaw's play *Pygmalion* opened at His Majesty's Theatre, London.

1915

Dardanelles Campaign in which British and Empire forces failed in their objectives to capture Constantinople, but incurred 220,000 casualties.

First zeppelin raid on London.

Douglas Haig appointed the new British Expeditionary Force Commander.

RMS *Lusitania* torpedoed by U-boat U-20 with a loss of 1,198 lives.

1916

Britain introduced conscription. Six million men were conscripted to fight.

Battle of the Somme in which the British army suffered its worst one-day combat losses in history, with nearly 60,000 casualties. The battle finally resulted in 623,907 British casualties. The result was indecisive. The tank was first used in this battle.

RAMC's first successful blood transfusion using blood that had been cooled and stored.

Lloyd George became Prime Minister.

Cinema audiences reached 20 million with 5,000 purpose-built cinemas.

Popular recordings included 'O Sole Mio' and 'Santa Lucia' by Enrico Caruso.

1917

Battle of Passchendaele in which British losses are estimated to have been between 200,000 and 448,614. 5 miles of new territory were gained (2 inches per dead soldier).

USA declared war on Germany.

Electric washing machines introduced to the UK from USA.

1918

First World War ended in November: total military and civilian casualties estimated as 16.5 million deaths and 21 million wounded.

1.1 million deaths and two million wounded amongst British Imperial Forces.

General Election won by the Liberal Party under David Lloyd George.

Worldwide influenza pandemic in which 228,000 UK citizens died.

Fisher Act made secondary education compulsory up to the age of 14.

The first national qualifications for England and Wales were introduced. The School Certificate Examination was taken at 16 and the Higher School Certificate at 18.

Women over the age of 30 allowed to vote.

Life expectancy for boys was 44 years and 50 years for girls.

Marie Stopes published a guide to contraception called *Wise Parenthood*. The book was strongly opposed by Anglican and RC church leaders.

37% of women in full-time employment.

1919

Paris Peace Conference.

Treaty of Versailles signed.

RAF formed by amalgamation of RFC and RNAS.

Nancy Astor elected and became the first woman to take her seat in the House of Commons (Constance Markievicz had been elected in 1918 but refused to take her seat in parliament as a protest against British policy in Ireland).

More tobacco sold as cigarettes than any other form of tobacco.

Invention of pop-up toaster.

1920

League of Nations formed in Paris.

The number of miners employed in UK peaked at 1·25 million.

First World Scout Jamboree held at Olympia, London.

First appearance of Hercule Poirot, Agatha Christie's moustachioed detective, in *The Mysterious Affair at Styles*.

D H Lawrence published *Women in Love*.

Enter Rupert Bear as a cartoon character in the *Daily Express*, created by Mary Tourtel.

Publication of *The Story of Doctor Dolittle* by Hugh Lofting.

1921

The province of Northern Ireland was created under the Government of Ireland Act.

Marie Stopes established the first birth control clinic in Holloway, London.

The first standard design telephone box arrived on the streets of Britain.

Launch of the Atco motor mower. 900 machines made in 1921 but this soon rose to tens of thousands.

Car tax discs introduced.

1922

General Election won by the Conservatives with Bonar Law as PM.

First radio news in UK presented by Arthur Burrows from newly formed British Broadcasting Company Ltd.

First radio broadcast of *Children's Hour* which ran until 1964.

Enid Blyton published her first book *Child Whispers*.

Richmal Crompton published the first William book, *Just William*. The books were adapted for radio in the 1940s.

1923

General Election resulted in a hung parliament. The Conservatives won the most seats but James Ramsay MacDonald became the PM.

British railways were grouped into the Big Four: LNER, GWR, SR and LMSR.

Matrimonial Causes Act established equal rights of divorce for men and women.

Several notable firsts in broadcasting by BBC: first outside broadcast, first broadcast of the chimes of Big Ben, first edition of *Radio Times*.

Explosion of recordings in USA by African American musicians such as Louis Armstrong and Jerry Roll Morton.

1924

General Election won by the Conservatives with Stanley Baldwin as PM.

Morris Motor Company became largest car manufacturer in UK.

Dora Russell and friends formed the Workers' Birth Control Group.

Married women banned from working in Civil Service. The ban lasted until 1946.

Margaret Bondfield became the first female Government Minister in the Ministry of Labour.

JAMES EDWARDS
James Edwards was born in Liverpool in June 1903

I was born in a quiet corner of Liverpool known as St Michael's in the Hamlet, but neither of my parents were Liverpudlians. My father had been brought up on a farm in Herefordshire, not far from Bromyard. Farming in Herefordshire had been a family tradition for at least four generations but my grandfather's early death had led to the dispersal of the family. My father started work at a young age in a butcher's shop in Upton-upon-Severn owned by two uncles, but in his early twenties set off to Liverpool to ply his trade in the city of opportunity. My mother's family came from the Isle of Man and her earliest memory was the sight of the steamer leaving Douglas Pier taking her parents in search of the 'brave new world'. Her parents soon established a fishmongers business in Liverpool where she later joined them, working in the shop until her marriage.

I grew up in a large family with two sisters and five brothers, although my elder brother, John, was killed in action during the First World War. In addition there were uncles and aunts not far away with whom I stayed from time to time. I can remember staying with my Aunts Polly and Bess and sitting up in bed alongside my sister Elsa and being shown off to some visitors by the light of an oil lamp.

From our home it was a short walk to the shore of the River Mersey and I must have played there as a child. This was known as the 'cast iron' shore because the iron used in the construction of the church had been cast there. A short walk in the opposite direction brought one to the now notorious Sefton Park. One childhood memory is of accompanying the pram to the park in charge of a nursemaid. Going down some steps the pram up-kicked and the contents fell out and I was held to be responsible. Sefton Park harbours an enormous glasshouse known as the Palm House, a huge circular domed affair. The atmosphere inside was always hot and steamy and the centre-piece was like an enclosed pond. The pond was probably only inches deep but I had a horror of its murky depths, from which grew tropical plants and ferns.

I can also remember attending a party in Myrtle Street. The journey would have entailed two tram journeys and so the decision was made to go in a horse-drawn vehicle. I chiefly remember the coloured jellies shivering in their dishes and the brightly coloured crackers made of a type of shiny translucent paper through which I peered at the gaslight in order to enjoy the full beauty of the glorious reds and blues.

Most of my childhood was spent in Wallasey on the other shore of the Mersey and my clearest recollections are associated with the Christmas festivities when there were a series of unmistakeable signs and portents. Probably the first was the Parish Magazine, which came out at the beginning of December and included appropriate Christian themes. My mother was a magazine distributor, but we minions did the distribution and I once had the misfortune to step off my bicycle without keeping hold of the handlebars and landed in a heap along with 'the Mags' as we called them. One of the recipients was a Mrs Coleman and her son, a school master, was a cricketer in one of the local teams that played in the Central Park, Wallasey. He wore a magnificent blazer and was good looking withal. Alas, he perished in France a few years later. Another house I called at, this must have been 1915/16, I remember being asked in, probably while they found the coppers to pay for the magazine. There was a photograph of a young man in military uniform, the frame all draped in black.

So much for the onset of Christmas. The next 'swallow' to arrive was the Almanack, given away by the *Liverpool Daily Post and Mercury,* as it was then known, which had a central picture surrounded by the calendar and sundry information such as postal charges. This had its hour of glory and was then destined to hang on the back of the door of the outside WC. Next in order would be Bunny's Christmas catalogue.

Bunny's were a well known city emporium specialising in ladies wear but other things as well and after going through all the dull clothes in the catalogue you eventually came to the toy section. O Boy! What joy! Lovely pictures of clockwork train sets and so forth. These pictures beguiled me for hours.

Even better things lay ahead. My Uncle Bob was a successful grocer in Whitchurch. Each year he sent us a hamper containing a cheese, a Melton Mowbray pie, mincemeat, and most particularly a splendid box of crackers. Finally Aunty Polly and Aunty Bess came over to Wallasey as they must have done to our Liverpool home, but it is their visits to Wallasey that I remember best. Their gifts were always munificent and on one occasion they sent us a kind of miniature billiard table, quite a handsome affair, which was hinged so that it could fold up and take less space. It was placed on the dining room table when we wanted to play. Considering they had no experience of children other than ourselves these two aunts go down in my book as somewhat approaching sainthood for the happiness they gave us. My brother Austin used to like to do their hair and would take it down and carefully pin it all up again. Not many women would put up with that sort of thing, I imagine.

At the time I speak of I was a choirboy and the season of Advent has ever since been my favourite part of the Christian Year. All of course confused with the secular side of things, but basically the message of the coming of Christmas linked with the coming of a better, happier world. In this connection I shall never forget the reading of one of the Advent Gospels which runs 'But what went ye out for to see …' We had at one time an Irish curate and I can still hear him saying 'Phwat' or something like that and each year as that Gospel is read I hear Noel Waring saying 'Phwat went ye out for to see'. As Christmas drew nearer we rehearsed carols and so the feeling of anticipation mounted in intensity. My sister Doris made decorative balls from crepe paper by sewing a series of dart like missiles on a string which ended up like a ball, I don't know how, and these were suspended from the gas bracket on either side of the dining room fireplace. Then there was the tree, a natural one, of course, with its tinsel and baubles and numerous small candles.

All this time my mother would be preparing mincemeat, plum pudding and bun loaf. This latter was made well in advance, I suppose. The other things were also but the bun loaves were wrapped in tea cloths and stowed away in the bottom drawer of a chest. No stainless steel in those days so each Saturday saw the knife board come out and the silver had to be cleaned. The latter was done with a mixture of ammonia and a white powder made into a paste. It made your eyes water and if you had a cut or chillblains, boy how the ammonia made them smart. But the same job before Christmas was done with twice the usual zest, although I always liked to get a good shine, especially on the steel knives. There was also a minor spring clean in which thankfully I was not involved.

Stockings were duly suspended and I don't remember ever being disappointed with the contents. The morning of Christmas Day was too wonderful to remember and of course we went to church to sing 'Christians Awake'. Christmas dinner was a heart warming as well as a stomach replenishing affair and we always rose to poultry unless, maybe, we had to forgo a bird during the war when the mincemeat contained some odd ingredients such as raw carrot. I think it likely that the last time we all sat around the table was Christmas 1913 for by the following December my brother, John, was in the army and we saw very little of him from then on. The climax of the meal was the pudding with blue flames from the burning brandy and sparklers and crackers. The latter remind me of one or two other adventitious items. The local grocer was rather 'up market' as we say now and so outside my mother's purse but I derived enormous pleasure from one of his shop windows, which was entirely given over to a wonderful display of boxes of crackers: a joy to behold. My mother regarded them as a wasteful extravagance so when I started to earn a living I took it upon myself to provide a box. Now I am inclined to share my mother's point of view, much as I enjoy their decorative contribution to a party. The mottoes, or whatever you call the literary content, had to be read out and enjoyed by all. On these occasions my father read the riot act if anyone began to eat before all were served. There were, as I suppose in any large family, the occasional mishaps and on one occasion my brother Eric, had received a gun of some kind that

The Edwards brothers (circa 1915).
Back row: (left) James, Cecil, and Eric. Front row: Geoffrey and Austin.

fired a missile tipped with a sucker which he aimed at a picture and shattered the glass. Mention of the gun reminds me of another shop, a toyshop this time, which had a special display at Christmas time and I used to press my nose against the window as I admired the contents. Mostly of a military nature, I fear. The guns were beautifully made by a firm named 'Brittain'. Generally speaking, with the outbreak of war, the quality of toys, especially clock work toys, deteriorated sadly and even as a boy I knew that 'Made in Germany' was a *sine qua non* for excellence.

On Boxing Day we went more often than not to a pantomime in Liverpool. I think I would have preferred to have remained at home. What I didn't like was coming home to a cold house, the fires having gone out and nothing left but bed. The message was clear, Christmas is over, and I felt sad, sad, sad.

New Years Day was but a pale reflection of the glories of Noel. We were allowed to stay up late as we grew older to let the New Year in and listen to the ships in dock or on the River Mersey, all sounding their sirens, quite a racket which endured for some minutes. In 1983 there are not enough ships around to make any sort of a noise. The day was enlivened by Yuletide fare. Calendars were hung up, new diaries received, their first entries made e.g. size of shoes, collars, etc. I was never a good diarist and although I derived great pleasure from their pristine purity and clean smell, my enthusiasm waned fairly soon and finally evaporated completely. Years later, I learned of a boy with a similar attitude to diary keeping whose entries more often than not ran 'forgot what did'. Probably the answer was 'nothing'.

James Edwards attended Wallasey Grammar School but had to leave at the age of seventeen following the death of his father, a source of great regret. He obtained employment with Martins Bank and worked for most of his life in their head office in Liverpool. He married Joan Bennion and they had three children, John, Richard and Janet. James was a very keen cyclist and walker and enjoyed classical music.

JOAN EDWARDS

Joan Edwards, née Bennion, was born in Woofferton, Shropshire, in November 1911.

I was born on the Shropshire end of the railway platform in the remote rural station of Woofferton, where my father was the stationmaster. The house was built right on the station and had a large garden, which seemed absolutely enormous to me as a little girl. It was wonderful countryside all around with the High Vennals on the one side and Clee Hill in the distance on the other. The garden was full of fruit trees, apples and damsons, and I had a swing from one of the damson trees where I used to spend many happy hours. We also had a number of filbert nut trees and I used to climb into the branches and crack the nuts with my teeth. I also used to eat the sharp Bramley apples with no ill results. There was a large station yard and outside our front gate was a wooden bar about six feet long where people used to tether their horses whilst they were at the station. There was a large warehouse with a platform round an oblong opening where a horse and cart could be backed in to unload and it had a small crane for lifting things. I was able to go and play in the warehouse. On the far side was a coal yard and also a timber yard and there was always a succession of horses and drays coming down. Nearby there was a little hut and a flat weighing machine where the loaded drays were weighed. I remember one day going into the hut where the man was a friend of mine, he was called Peter Hamilton, but talking to him was a large black man. He was the first black man I had ever seen. Mr Hamilton asked if I would like to give him a kiss and I remember flying home in the most terrible panic.

All the horses that came into the yard were a great joy to me and I longed for a horse of my own. I can remember that I used to put my little clenched fist into the steaming nostrils of the large cart horse to feel the hot breath, and I used to play a game of my own which consisted of bending and running under the horse's belly. One of the neighbours once told my mother about it and she said she would rather not know. When I say neighbours, there was a row of about six cottages on the far side of the station yard and a small pub on the corner that was referred to as 'the Boozer'. One of

Joan in the garden at Woofferton (circa 1915).

the houses had some children about my age and I sometimes played with a girl called Alice Wright but it was not encouraged as they were considered a bit down the social scale. These cottages had communal loos at the end of the yard for the lot of them. Another clear recollection one Christmas is seeing three geese hanging by their feet with their throats cut, left to die. They were trying to suck up the blood as it ran from their throats. The sight has never left me and must have been horrific for a small child, but that is how they did it in those days.

I can remember that I was once so desperate for a horse that I got up on one of the drays having undone the horse and started to drive it across the yard. As it happened I had chosen a blind horse. To my horror I found that I couldn't stop it and I could see the sawmill gates coming nearer and nearer. Anyway a happy ending. One of the men saw what was happening and ran and caught the horse's bridle just as it reached the gate, and I didn't get told off too badly either.

My sister Mabel (Maim) and I were born at home and it was a nice three bedroomed house with a drawing room, which was only used on high days and holidays. The kitchen was only small and our lighting was oil lamps and candles. There was no bathroom but my bedroom had a bath in it, which was connected to a cold tap. All hot water had to be heated on the fire and carried upstairs if one wanted a bath, so it was once a week in those days. I can remember distinctly, when I was in the kindergarten in Ludlow, the teacher asking us how many baths we had each week. Most of the children replied 'every night' or 'every other night' but me, being honest piped up 'once a week'. The teacher was horrified and more or less proclaimed me a dirty pig in front of the whole class.

When I was five years old I joined my sister at the Bluecoat School in Hereford but I only remained there for one term. I was very unhappy there and remember crying all the first day and not really knowing what it was all about. The school sent a message to my mother asking her to teach me my sums but I could never understand why two and two should make four, and I haven't learned much since. I also remember taking large amounts of sawdust to school to stuff some dolls we had made but was not allowed to stuff mine because my stitches were so large and sawdust would have come through. I remember feeling how unjust it was that I had supplied the stuff and not been given any!

As I hated it so much, and the girls used to frighten me with ghost stories on the train journey I was taken away and sent to a Dame School at Brimfield. The two 'dames' had this lovely old house in a wonderful garden and taught a small bunch of children where I don't suppose we learned anything at all. We did 'cup hooks' and 'coat hangers' which may have been the beginning of my handwriting. However, it seems to be the injustices that I remember. We were told to write a letter to our mothers. I was able to do this but I did not start 'Dear Mother' because we did not call her mother but 'Movie'. So I wrote 'Dear Movie'. I was hauled over the coals for not being able to spell 'mother'.

When I was six or seven I was sent to join my sister who had obtained a scholarship for Ludlow High School and I started in 'Transition' with a horrible teacher called Miss Walters. I can only remember three things: making blue clay beads for a bracelet, making an oasis with palm trees and the third is painting a picture and being told how lovely it was. I remember replying modestly, 'Oh, it isn't really,' and the teacher reacted by saying, 'Well in that case we will not hang it on the wall.'

My mother had a friend called Mrs Yapp and I think they owned a smallholding near to Orleton. About once a year we were taken for a ride in Mr Yapp's trap, which must have been a great honour as he was a surly little man. It was a tall trap and the passengers sat in the back: nothing so smart as a governess cart. I suppose because we had no transport I did not see a great deal of the surrounding countryside apart from what I could see from railway carriage windows, the occasional trap ride and walks. I did have a little bicycle but don't remember that we ever went for bike rides. I used to ride it round and round the goods yard and occasionally over the bridge towards Orleton, but I was not allowed to go any further.

The Yapps always had a hay making period in the hot summer weather and on a certain day we would be invited up there to help hay make. My mother used to say that they used her as an unpaid labourer as the hay had to be tossed and turned and loaded on to a wagon. We used to have a marvellous time rolling about in the hay and there was always a picnic tea in the hay field.

Corn cutting was quite a business in those days because all these jobs were done with horses and old fashioned farm implements. I can particularly remember one occasion of a field of corn cut near our home. The reaper had gone round and round the field until there was a small area remaining in the centre with the corn still standing. All the local people were about. When it came to the final few rounds all the rabbits would rush out of the still-standing corn and this would be the sign for the guns to go off and for people to throw sticks and try to club them. It was just one of those things that always happened in a cornfield.

The greatest event of the year was the May Fair. There used to be one in Hereford and one in Ludlow. Remember there were no cars. Everyone from far and wide would converge on the two towns at the appropriate time and I expect those people who came by horse and trap would leave them at a hostelry. The whole of the town was taken over with a real fair, including hurdy-gurdy horses, chair-o-planes and swinging boats. Rows and rows of all kinds of tents and stalls filled all the streets for some days. I loved the horses roundabout the best and always tried to get an outside horse. There were stalls selling

Joan (right) and her sister Mabel, known as Maim (circa 1926).

gingerbread and sweets and all manner of wonderful things. The fair at Ludlow filled the square outside the castle and outside the high school and went all along the main street and turned the town into a fairyland for children.

I never received any pocket money as a child, but I was occasionally given the odd penny or halfpenny. Of course in those days you could buy a lot for a penny. There was one special shop in Ludlow where I used to stand with my nose glued to the window. It was full of sweets such as liquorice bootlaces and sherbet bags and it was an agonising process trying to decide what the precious penny should be spent on. It was also possible to buy a halfpenny ice cream and sometimes when I was wealthy I purchased one of these.

Joan Edwards was a stationmaster's daughter and lived firstly at Woofferton and then Hooton stations. She left school at the age of thirteen as her parents made unfavourable comparisons with her academically-gifted sister. She attended a secretarial college in Liverpool and worked for a number of organisations, including Martins Bank. After raising her family, John, Richard and Janet, she worked as a medical secretary until her early seventies. Joan was a great animal lover and a very enthusiastic motorist.

ARWYN JONES

Arwyn Jones was born in the village of Llangennech, Carmarthen, in July 1916.

I was born in the middle of the First World War. My parents were a very loving couple and their manner created a very happy and easy atmosphere in the home. My father had grown up on a farm and had a great love of animals but as the family was a large one he had to seek work elsewhere and obtained a surface job at a nearby colliery. My mother was a very keen herbalist and I remember that nettles often featured in her remedies. On one occasion I had a very painful ear ache which she treated by asking me to pee into a jar and then poured a few drops into my ear. I was astonished to find many years later when I was working as a pharmacist that urea drops were recommended in the British National Pharmacopoeia as a treatment for ear problems! We were dosed with sulphur (popularly known as brimstone) and treacle as a Spring tonic, supposedly to purify the blood and a purgative such as Senna was given at weekends. It was a very happy house and my parents' lives were devoted entirely to the family.

Families were generally much larger in those days than they are today and I was the youngest of five boys. I believe I was an afterthought because my eldest brother, Oswald, was nineteen years older than me. Oswald was very keen on aviation and at the time that I was born he was on war service as a flying officer pilot in the Royal Flying Corps. I understand that his work was mainly reconnaissance and he had a 'spotter' with a camera. He carried with him a Winchester repeating rifle, but I don't know if he ever used it. I recall that Oswald had fixed a large propeller to the wall in one of the living rooms.

Our house was one of a cluster of cottages situated on the slope of a not very steep mountain about one and a half miles outside the village of Llangennech in South Wales. This little group of houses was isolated from the village and conditions were somewhat primitive by today's standards. Mains water was not connected to the houses, but two pumps were placed in different parts of the road and whichever one of us boys had a spare moment would pick up one of the three or four cans (capacity I think about three or four gallons) fill it up with water and carry it back to the house. Although I cannot remember the age I was when we did have water connected to the house it was a great day of celebration.

Electricity was not installed until I was seven or eight years old up to which time lighting was by oil lamps. Going upstairs was by candlelight, as taking oil lamps was considered too dangerous. Once electricity was brought to the area and connected to the house my elder brother lost no time in wiring the whole house and our home became the 'showhouse' of the little community. Heating was by coal fires in the living rooms only, so the bedrooms were on the chilly side in the winter months.

Another exciting incident around that time was having a crystal radio. Initially it was with a single headphone so only one person could listen at one time. Some of us would gather around the person with the headphone trying to hear 'What is he saying?' Eventually we graduated to having a loud speaker and we could all enjoy it together. This was a great advance indeed!

In those times it was very common for people to own a piano and everyone used to gather at our house because it had such a happy atmosphere. My brother Cyril had a very fine bass-baritone voice and sang in the church choir. We used to have some lovely singsongs and Welsh hymns were always a popular choice.

Air travel was very much in its infancy so whenever we heard the sound of a plane we would dash outside and have a look at it. Looking back it was an exciting period with so many developments, such as improvement in transport with cars becoming more popular and people becoming much more mobile.

I attended the church school in the village until I went to the secondary school in the town of Llanelli, which was about four miles away. It was quite a long journey: the walk to the village, the bus dropping us off in the centre of the town and then an uphill walk to the school. We did not mind this at all as we were quite a happy little group plodding along together.

Arwyn Jones studied Pharmacy at London University. He practised as a pharmacist for most of his working life in Newbury, where he was a much respected and loved member of the community. He was married to Betty and they had two daughters, Pauline and Christine. Sadly Pauline and Betty have pre-deceased him. Arwyn continues to live in retirement in Newbury where his main pleasure is listening to classical music.

IVAN GEFFEN

Ivan Geffen was born in Fulham, London, in March 1920

I have no recollection of anything that happened during my first two years. My earliest memory is of myself standing on the grass in Kensington Gardens, beside a pram which contained my baby brother Terry who was born in Bradford in 1921. At that time dad was a school medical officer, having been invalided out of the RAMC as a Captain at the end of the Great War. To make sense of what happened later, I have to go back half a century before I was born.

My grandfather, John Lionel Geffen, was born in 1870 into a Jewish family in Vilkomir in Lithuania, which was then part of the Czarist empire. Anti-semitism was then State-sanctioned. It was rife and often murderously violent. John Lionel and his younger sister Gittel became refugees, arriving in London in the late 1880s. I remember meeting her once, when I was taken to her little wine-bottling shop in Whitechapel. I remember the handle-operated machine which inserted corks into the newly filled bottles. My great-aunt wore dark clothes and seemed to be quite old. When we left she gave me an apple. This was my first personal contact with the Jewish East End of London. The second was in the late 1930s, when Richard Crown (a fellow student) arrived at University College with his head bandaged. Leaving his home in Whitechapel to come to College, he had been attacked by some of Sir Oswald Moseley's Blackshirts.

When he arrived in England my Grandpa Geffen spoke Hebrew, Yiddish and Russian, and possibly German. By my time, he spoke fluent English, but with a German accent. His family name was probably pronounced Gayfan, which translates into English as the grape vine. Biblical Hebrew is written without vowels. He had adapted his name to the nearest he could get in English, and Geffen we have remained throughout the English-speaking world. By contrast great-aunt Gittel continued to speak Yiddish, and almost no English, until she died.

My grandfather had a very good memory and a good, light tenor voice. He could recite, and chant, the whole of the Torah (the five books of Moses in Hebrew, which together form the beginning of the Old Testament). After he arrived in England he must have acquired the skills and knowledge needed to be appointed as a chazan (synagogue cantor). During my early years he was the chazan of the New West End synagogue in Bayswater. The elaborately dressed scrolls on each of which the Torah is written were kept, when not in use, in the synagogue ark. Every Sabbath the ark was opened and he carried one of the scrolls to the amemah (a raised enclosure in the centre of the synagogue), removed the scroll's dress and opened the scroll at the point which had been reached at the previous reading. Then he read and recited the part of the Torah which was allocated to that day.

All five of my grandparents' children attended London public schools. I have no idea how this was financed, but the synagogue served a relatively wealthy congregation. It may be that although a chazan's salary was small, funds were made available for school fees and that the Ministers' houses were provided free of rent.

I remember Grandpa Geffen as an old gentleman who wore a black suit and a black top hat. These were part of his Sabbath appearance, but such an outfit was by no means unusual at that time. It 'went with' several occupations and activities well into the 1930s. When we went to Grandpa and Grandma Geffen's house for lunch (I think on Saturdays), he followed the meal by rolling a cigarette. He then halved it and smoked one half. Theirs must have been an unorthodox household. In addition to my grandparents it consisted of my Uncle Leonard (the youngest of their three surviving sons) and their housekeeper Miss May. Although a Christian, she was thoroughly judaized. She took part in the Passover feasts. More to my point, she cooked the Saturday lunch. This was clearly contrary to the commandment which requires Jews to make the Sabbath a day of rest for their employees as well as for themselves.

The next event, which I recall distinctly, followed soon after Grandpa Geffen's death and led to the beginning of my understanding of what it is to be a Jew. My father had succeeded his father as head of the Geffen family. In this role he and my mother hosted what was to become my first Passover (Seder) and as the youngest male present I had to ask the Four Questions. My father taught me the words and the accompanying chant. They began 'Daddee' (the second syllable was stressed and lengthened), 'I want to ask you four questions. The first question is, "Wherefore is this night distinguished from all other nights?"' This, and the following questions, were answered by my father with similar formality and summarised the story of the Jews' bondage as slaves in Egypt under a Pharaoh who knew not Joseph, of God's command through the Jewish leader Moses that every Jewish household should sprinkle on its threshold the blood of a newly slaughtered lamb, of how the Angel of Death flew over the whole of the land of Egypt and (sparing only the blood-protected Jewish households) took the firstborn in every family, including their livestock, and of how Moses led his people to and across the Red Sea, in which the pursuing Egyptian army drowned. It is a terrible story, the first Holocaust of which I have knowledge. The memory of this story, and of the need to rejoice in its outcome, can move me to tears to this day.

Also disturbing, in my boyhood, at every Seder we used ritually to hope that although this year we were in a strange land, next year we would be in Israel. Many of us now grieve for the way in which the modern state of Israel treats many of its subjects.

When the Jews fled from Egypt, they left in desperate haste. They had no time to leaven the dough which was baking in their ovens. What they took with them was unleavened bread (matzoh) and to this day in every orthodox Jewish household the Passover is preceded by ritual cleaning to remove every trace of food or drink which might contain yeast. In such households there are separate services of dishes and cutlery which are used eight days only in every year. Everything has to be kosher al pesach (clean enough for Passover). For the Passover feast the table carries a lamb bone and other reminders of our history. At the feast a place is set, and kept free (as is a portion of matzoh), for Elijah. If he arrives to announce the coming of the Messiah, there will be a suitable welcome for him. After the feast traditional family songs are sung.

I have no religious belief. It is more than half a century since I took part in a seder and even longer since the time when I could read and follow the text of the service in Hebrew. Nonetheless, everything I have just written is part of my living memory. Belief is not a necessary part of being a Jew.

Our persecutors have made the Jews into a race of survivors. Those who remain are descended from those who had the cunning, the physique, the skill or the luck to survive adversity. This is not a matter of virtue or morality and few people positively choose the qualities which ensure their own or their descendants' survival. Some, when barred by a ruler or by local custom from following many occupations, became cobblers, tailors, and moneylenders. Most people need money, clothes and footwear. Others have been actors, musicians, boxers and artists. Collectively, we are what others have made of us.

In various ways, that was an eventful time in my life. I contracted an infection and was sent to a convalescent home, where I promptly contracted something worse. My father, who was a GP, thought it was diphtheria. I know four things about it. I had to stay in bed for several weeks. While in bed I pretended to write connected 'small' letters. I learnt how to tell the time. Towards the end, being bored, I got out of bed and promptly collapsed on the floor, my leg muscles having wasted through lack of use.

In 1924 my parents took Terry and me and Grandma Geffen to Knokke on the Belgian coast. There were sand dunes. This may have been my first experience of sand. On the sea front was a row of shops. In front of one of them stood a display of shining objects. No-one would tell me what they were. They were shell cases from the World War, which had ended five and a half years earlier. Once, in a café, dad was playing a form of billiards. I was fascinated by the lump of chalk which he applied to his cue and when we left the café the chalk was in my pocket. It was soon retrieved

This was also the year in which I gained my first awareness of politics. My father was a member of the ILP (Independent Labour Party) and the Herald was our daily paper. The first Labour government was forced into a second General Election in the same year. During it, the Tory press ran an entirely fictitious story of the Zinoviev Red Letter, claiming that Labour depended on Soviet communist gold. This typically dishonest trick worked. Labour lost office and power and although it won again in 1929, it was brought down by the Wall Street crash of 1931.

Going back to the mid-twenties. I was then too young to know where dad stood in the political spectrum. He was certainly somewhere in the main stream of the Labour Party. He was once Labour candidate in Kensington for the LCC (London County Council) and for six years in the 1930s he was a Labour councillor, representing the Golborne Ward on Kensington Borough Council. That was a slum ward and that was a time when I recall seeing local children barefoot in our street, wearing only two garments. As I grew up, I knew which side our family was on.

Before our school days, Terry and I were almost daily walkers in Kensington Gardens. With a nanny or governess we walked about a mile to High Street, Notting Hill Gate, and from there to the park. Its entrance was near the southern end of Queen's Road. We walked, sometimes to Kensington Palace, sometimes to the adjacent Dutch (or Sunken) Garden and sometimes to the Round Pond. Later, when school precluded daily walking, we walked at weekends to Hyde Park Corner, a round trip of six miles. Sometimes we took a one penny bus ride to Exhibition Road and walked down it to the Science or the Natural History Museum, both of which became familiar haunts.

In 1926 Terry and I ceased to spend virtually all our time together. Each morning I was taken a short distance along a neighbouring road to the house where the Misses Ford ran a kindergarten. In the short time that I spent there, with other children I played with toy money and assembled a wooden jigsaw puzzle each of whose pieces represented a European country. The boundaries of Poland, Yugoslavia and Czechoslovakia were relatively new, even to adults. At around the same time, at William Whiteley's department store in Queen's Road, I experienced my first Armistice Day, 11 November, when everyone stood silent and still for two minutes at eleven o'clock in the morning.

The same store was also the scene of one of my first remembered disappointments. Terry and I were taken to the grotto where Father Christmas was reached by a coach, which carried a dozen or more children. At its front was a bell, which was operated by the one child who got to the right place at the right time. I desperately wanted to be the bell ringer, but in vain.

There was still a governess, part of whose job was to mount home theatricals, in which Terry and I played Little Red Riding Hood and the Wolf and similar shows. Dad also taught us the elements of boxing, which we once performed at a fair in aid of a Jewish charity, in an enormous house in what may still be known as millionaires' row, near Kensington Gardens.

Dad had a large and varied library, much of which dated back to his boyhood. His favourite authors included H G Wells, Jack London, Conan Doyle and Edgar Wallace. Terry and I became enthusiastic readers.

After the governesses there came a succession of au pairs. One of these was French and very strict. She may have been a good teacher, but Terry and I did not like her and were glad when she left. Two were German. Their background and ideas were similar to those of our parents and they were very much loved. They introduced us to Kartoffelbrei (a wonderful potato dish) and to Skat (pronounced skaht), which is a card game for three players, using a double pack from which all cards from six down have been withdrawn.

They taught us some French and German and to understand something of how these languages are written and pronounced. We also learnt to play chess and draughts, and adult visitors to the house sometimes played against us. We played other mind games, such as Pelmanism, and later Aviation and Dover Patrol. These are first class mind trainers and I am sorry that their day seems to have ended seventy or more years ago. Dad bought a glass-blowing set, followed by a chemistry set and an electricity set. He showed us how to carry out the various experiments (and no-one was hurt). By the time I was about ten I could assemble and understood the working of an electric bell and had some understanding of the working of a telephone.

From the kindergarten I moved to Porchester House School, a preparatory school near Paddington station. I spent five terms there. I had my first experience of bullying by larger, tougher boys. I must have talked endlessly. One visitor to the house said, 'Ivan talks too much', which was probably true but still unkind. Terry was remembered as saying 'Schooerl, schooerl, schooerl. I'm tired of schooerl, schooerl, schooerl.'

In September 1928 Terry and I both started at another preparatory school, Devon House, to which we could walk from our house. There were three teachers: Dudley Gill (head), Mr Fison and Miss Burns. Terry says that when we arrived, there were only eleven boys. He is probably right, but I think that there were more, not least because the economics of setting up a new school do not justify employing three people to teach eleven children with an age range of seven to twelve.

I was Geffen One and Terry was Geffen Two. Each school day began with prayers in number one form room. Terry and I and the other one or two Jewish boys stood outside the room until prayers were over. I do not know what the other boys made of this division. As the number of boys grew, Mr Gill divided us into Drake House and Raleigh House. He encouraged competition. The houses competed at cricket and football (I was clumsy and inept at both). We competed for good conduct marks, five of which were awarded at the beginning of each term to anyone who could recite correctly and in sequence the names and dates of English sovereigns from William I to George V. I learnt these once and started each term with a five mark lead.

We competed in other ways. When I supported Cambridge in the Boat Race, Terry supported Oxford. Having been born in Bradford, he adopted Yorkshire as 'his' cricket team. Not very enthusiastically, I supported Middlesex.

Useless at sport and athletics, I did well in class. Latin and Mathematics came easily to me, as did any exercise of memory. Although I did not know it until I was in Normandy in 1944, I am a natural linguist. In my first term at Devon House Mr Gill assigned to us the parts that we were to perform in *The Tempest,* towards the end of term. As Miranda I was the 'female' lead and had the most lines to learn with the possible exception of Prospero. There is no reason to suppose that I was a good or convincing actor, but I probably looked the part. In the following years I was Martha Cratchit, Sebastian and Orlando. At eleven I threw the wrestler Charles, showed compassion for the aged Adam and (for the first of many times) fell in love with Rosalind. I never had a problem with my lines.

As you may have noticed, girls are almost entirely absent from my story. The truth is that they were almost entirely absent from my life. I had eight girl cousins but we did not see them very often and anyway, boys played with boys and girls played with girls. I knew almost nothing about gender differences and supposed that these lay mainly in the fact that girls wore dresses and their hair was cut differently. I was thirteen or fourteen before sex and I became even moderately acquainted.

My parents were both music lovers, a chief interest being in Wagner's operas. When I was about eight they made changes in the arrangement of the house, so that the large first floor living room became the music room, with a baby grand piano and a wind-up gramophone. At six shillings (thirty pence) each, records of classical music were expensive. They were also fragile, easily scratched and broken. The record collection grew slowly. A single disc represented a substantial outlay. The Schubert C major quintet occupied six records, which I set about buying one at a time (in my late teens).

At ten I was an enthusiastic Wagnerite and was familiar with parts of several of his operas. Once, I got into trouble with Mr Gill when at school I argued that great composers were more heroic (an unfortunate choice of word, as I soon realised) than great soldiers. Before Maia took me to my first orchestral concert, Florence Austral's farewell, at the Queen's Hall in Upper Regent Street, when I was ten years old I knew that total silence was required during the performance. At the same age I saw Parsifal, Faust and Hansel and Gretel. I was a privileged child.

Dad had a relatively small 'private' practice, the patients of which paid two shillings and sixpence to see him in his consulting room, on the ground floor of our house. He had a surgery between our house and Portobello Road, which was then a sizeable street market, and spent long evenings there, returning home late, except on Thursdays, when there was no evening surgery. Employed men were able to join a GP's panel list. The GP received an annual fee (less than a pound) for each patient who was on his 'panel' list. I believe that dad had between 1,200 and 1,800 panel patients.

On Thursday evenings our parents went to one of the many theatres in the West End. Terry and I were first taken to the theatre to see Peter Pan when I was about four. Our parents were careful to ensure that we knew the story before we went. Despite my reservations I joined in the applause when Tinker Bell was poisoned and Peter told us that she would survive only if all of us showed that we believed in fairies by clapping our hands in applause. A year or two later we saw 'Where the Rainbow Ends'.

I have mentioned some early disappointments. I shall add another. In the early years, like other middle class children, we received generous quantities of books and toys at Christmas. I think it was at the end of 1928 that we went as a family to holiday at the Mermaid Hotel in Rye (Sussex). The weather was cold and snowy, but there was a big blazing log fire in the guests' lounge. It did not surprise us that the hotel did not shower gifts on us. The shock came when we returned home to a house which had been unheated for several days, and in which there was not a single present for either of us. Our parents celebrated the Jewish festivals. Christmas just did not count. I doubt whether either of them was ever aware of our disappointment.

In term time, my daily life was quite strenuous. Terry and I were up, dressed, fed and on our way to school before our parents got up. On two afternoons a week the school staff took us to a playground in Ealing for cricket or football. We spent five mornings and three afternoons in class. Save at the very beginning, part of every evening in the week was spent doing homework. Preparatory schools existed for one reason: to get boys into public schools. There was (and is) a hierarchy of these. The fees charged are sometimes enormous and act as a safety barrier to exclude almost all boys whose parents are not very rich. Entrance to the lower-ranked public schools was usually via the Common Entrance exam. Competitive scholarship examinations enabled the public schools to achieve their historic function of educating 'poor scholars' who were to be included among the country's future leaders and rulers.

So, although I was scarcely aware of it, my four years at Devon House were a time of grooming for scholarship examinations, and for public school life.

I was always asking questions. When I was ten, standing beside the family car, I asked dad 'If God made everything, who made God?' I received no answer. In this respect dad was an honest man. Although I did not know it at the time, this was a critical moment in the making of the person I am. For over eighty years, when not an agnostic, I have been an atheist.

Ivan Geffen attended Westminster School and studied Law at London University. During the Second World War he served in the Royal Artillery but later transferred to the Army Educational Corps. In 1959 he established his own legal practice in Walsall, which became one of the first predominantly legal aid practices in the country. Ivan was a Labour candidate in five general elections. Ivan has been married three times. Ivan and Mary Geffen have between them eighteen grandchildren plus great-grandchildren.

TED BARTON
Ted Barton was born in Acton
(now Ealing W3) in September 1923

I was born into a family which prospered on the foundations of my grandparents' financial success. My father's father was a successful laundry owner and his claim to fame was having introduced soap powder to this country. My mother's father had worked for many years as a 'waterman and lighterman' and had done very nicely from his various dealings. He had the habit whenever we met of giving me a 'penny' which usually turned out to be a sovereign, which was hastily confiscated by my mother 'in case I lost it'.

At the age of two and a half reports have it that I was stricken with double pneumonia and pleurisy, a serious situation and I was considered to be at death's door for some time. My memories are naturally rather hazy, but I can visualise a small bed downstairs in a corner of the dining room. Naturally this child, me, was considered to have a weak chest and dubious stamina for many years. It therefore came as something of a shock to my parents when at the age of eighteen this weakling was declared A-one, physically fit to join the RAF aircrew. And here's an irony for you. The recruiting office where I joined up and had my medical was immediately across the road from where I had been so ill.

The little house where I was born was a 'starter home' for middle class families, possibly purchased for my parents as a wedding present. A few years later, presumably with increasing affluence, my parents decided to move to Ealing Common. This was not only a move to a larger house but a definite step up the social ladder. I have a very clear picture in my mind of travelling with my mother from one house to another on the tram, presumably my father was at work. Did the van 'follow after' or did it go before? The journey entailed a change of trams and a mile walk to the new house, which was new in every sense being part of an estate which was being built and for quite a long time houses were being constructed around us.

Due to the existence of the District Line at the bottom of our road, the roads adjacent to our houses were mainly cul de sacs and consequently there was no through traffic. This meant that the roads were safe places for young boys to play and many happy hours were spent by a little gang of local youngsters developing their skills of football and cricket. It seemed quite acceptable to collect misdirected balls from front gardens as long as it was not too frequent.

At the age of five I was sent off to the nearest local school, Hilsborough, about a mile and a half from home, across the busy main Uxbridge Road with its trams. Amazingly by the time I was six I was making this journey twice a day on my own. I do remember this quite clearly because at some stage between six and seven I was asked, no commanded, to take home a letter to my parents. You may ask why: well the exact reason escapes me but it was something to do with a misdemeanour of some sort, or perhaps a series of them. I remember thinking that if the letter never arrived my parents would be none the wiser, and retain their belief in their beloved son. No sooner was this reasoning reached than the letter was stuffed into a nearby hedge, and I went happily on my way. Needless to say when the school failed to receive any comment from my parents enquiries were made, and ultimately a confession was extracted from me. What discussions took place between my parents and the school I do not know, but at the end of the term I was moved to another establishment, Hamilton House School, where I remained with unsullied character for a number of years.

Perhaps here is a moment to digress into a few sartorial details. The uniform for most schools at that time was almost universal. Grey single-breasted jacket, grey knee-length socks and black lace-up shoes. The only variations that I can remember lay in the cap, which varied in colour from school to school and some schools affected a coloured band round the top of the socks. Added to this was an obligatory leather satchel as homework was part of life even at this early age. When I moved to Cranleigh the only variation was a blue blazer with a badge on the chest pocket, the colour depending on which 'House' you were attached to. Shorts continued until the fifth form when 'long trousers' were worn. Sweaters were worn according to the date rather than the temperature.

Back to Hamilton House School. Here again there was plenty of opportunity for schoolboy delights. After the initial few days of introduction I was allowed to go to and fro to school under my own steam. By this time I was the proud owner of a bike and this was my daily means of travel. Now between our house and the school was Ealing Common, a considerable area of grass with roads both around it and across it, but none of which led directly to school. In the minds of schoolboys the natural thing was to cycle across the common. Unfortunately this was forbidden by every by-law imaginable, so that for a number of years we waged a running battle with the park keeper who, if he caught us, would make us dismount, walk to the edge of the grass and continue our journey on the road. Looking back this was all done with a certain amount of good humour on both sides.

Ealing Common was also the site of a major fair, which was held twice a year and this was always located in a hollow within otherwise flat terrain. The first arrivals were enormous wagons, usually in pairs, pulled by equally enormous steam engines. If the weather remained dry for their stay of about a week all was well. With English weather it was rare for a completely dry week with the result that getting all this gear out of the hollow was a major undertaking. First the steam engines had to run out cables to the stout horse chestnut trees that lined the road and winch themselves up the slope, then anchoring themselves to a tree they had to winch the trailers up one by one. Each wagon as it came up created more mud and each had to find a temporary resting place until they were all up. Tempers frayed, language became more picturesque and the local small boys, including me, enjoyed the spectacle and found yet another excuse for being late home.

Another delight of the common for a bunch of football-mad boys was that with two coats for goalposts and a borrowed football many happy hours were passed, supposedly training for eventual inclusion in the school team and hopefully for the local team, Brentford. Oh! Happy dreams! Many were the 'tickings-off' for arriving home hours after the expected time. 'Late for tea again!' My dad was a stickler for time; even a few minutes was enough to produce some comment and, of course, muddy knees did not improve the shining hour.

It came to me the other day that I had missed out one of the almost anonymous characters that were present in 8, Evelyn Grove for many years and I refer of course to the maid. There was no 'one' of these since they came and went fairly regularly, usually at about yearly intervals. Mostly they were young girls, between fourteen and sixteen who lived their lives 'in service'. In the case of those who helped out in our house their conditions were peculiar by today's standards, but normal at the time. Each girl lived in and had her own bedroom, ate the same food as everyone else and had one afternoon and one evening off each week. However, certain conditions applied. Her bedroom did not have a washbasin with taps and drain, nor was she permitted to use the bathroom or toilet upstairs. So her washing water was taken upstairs in a large enamel jug and the used water carried down again. There was an outside toilet more or less reserved for her. Strangely enough my mother did almost all the cooking, though washing up was almost always for the maid. Each day one of the living rooms were scheduled for cleaning though here again my mother helped. Other duties included bringing the meals to the table, where dad carved and mum served the vegetables, clearing away and washing up. She was also responsible for laying and lighting the living room fire, making sure the hot water boiler was kept alight (a fearsome coke boiler) and ensuring the coal scuttles were full.

Only two of these girls stand out in my memory. The first was Dorothy who was with us for quite a few years. I remember spending quite a time in the kitchen during daytime, obviously in my early childhood, when she helped me with my writing and reading. She must have made good use of her afternoons off, because she left to get married. The other was Nellie who again was with us for a good many years: a large, rather ungainly girl but who was to become very much one of the family within a limited way. She remained with my parents even after I joined up in 1942 and finally left because she was directed into some form of war work.

About this time two items came into my life which were to be very much at the centre for many years, in fact one continued until very recently, these were an o-gauge Hornby railway and Meccano, both of fairly limited scope to start, but to grow over the years until my bedroom could hardly contain them. Part of this was my father's fault in that for Christmas one year, I think I was about nine, he managed to build for me, entirely secretly until the day, an enormous Meccano crane. It stood about three feet high with a horizontal jib beam along which the hook was able to move in and out. Eventually, of course, it was dismantled, and over the years became many other things.

The time between moving from my preparatory school to Cranleigh was one of 'great adventures', or so it seemed to me. Saturdays and Sundays were days mainly without any structure to them, so that my great pal, Robin Harbud, and I travelled miles on our bikes. It must be remembered that traffic was not so heavy as nowadays and probably slower moving too. It was for instance a great delight to catch up a lorry or a van and hold onto its tailboard for a free tow. Nearside mirrors were a rarity so we were seldom detected. Kew, Richmond and Kingston were regarded as normal destinations to the south and Uxbridge to the west. The north was less attractive since anywhere in that direction meant climbing the dreaded Hangar Hill, great speed and excitement coming back!

Whether the weather was more violent in those days I don't know but I can clearly remember quite often standing at home in the front window with my dad watching the most tremendous thunderstorms with enormous flashes of lightning and deafening thunder, whilst my mother urged us both, 'Come away from that window, you'll get struck in a minute!'

Ted Barton joined the RAF in 1942 and became a Flight Lieutenant. Much of his flying was carried out in Canada but one role was flying a glider during the final airborne landing in Germany. Ted decided at an early stage that the family laundry business was not to his taste and embarked on a life of amazing diversity. His career has included working as a GPO operator, chicken farmer, warden of a Cheshire Home, canal lock keeper and as a Baptist minister. He eventually became an Anglican priest and still conducts services in Cornwall. Ted was married twice, to Audrey and then Vonnie, both of whom have sadly predeceased him.

TIMELINE OF BRITISH SOCIAL HISTORY: 1925–1950

1925

    John Logie Baird gave first public demonstration of television.

    Clarence Birdseye invented a process for frozen food.

    Major American recording companies switched to electric microphone technology; one of the most important advances in recording technology.

    Married women who divorced their husbands were allowed to apply for custody of their children at all ages.

    Exposition Internationale des Arts Décoratifs et Industriels Modernes held in Paris. The exhibition had a major influence on architecture and industrial design in the 1930s.

1926

    General strike: between 1·5 and 1·7 million workers on strike. Martial law declared.

    Days lost by strikes peaked at 160 million.

    1·7 motor vehicles registered. 2·9 fatalities per thousand vehicles.

    Peak year for popularity of the Charleston dance.

    Popular recorded music included 'Bye Bye Blackbird' (Gene Austin) and 'When the Little Red Robin Goes Bob Bob Bobbin' Along' (Paul Whiteman and his orchestra).

    A A Milne published *Winnie-the-Pooh*.

1927
- First trans-Atlantic telephone call.
- Charles Lindbergh made the first solo non-stop flight across the Atlantic.
- Teddy Wakelam gave the first sports commentary on BBC Radio.
- First appearance of Agatha Christie's character 'Miss Marples', in a short story entitled *The Tuesday Night Club*.

1928
- Representation of the People's Act lowers the voting age for women from 30 to 21 giving them equal suffrage with men.
- Alexander Fleming discovered penicillin.
- Baird demonstrated colour television.
- First broadcast of 'Nine Lessons and Carols' from King's College, Cambridge.
- Release of first Walt Disney cartoon featuring Mickey Mouse in *Steamboat Willie*.
- Gracie Fields made her first records with 'I Love You' and 'My Blue Heaven'.

1929
- General Election in which the Labour Party gained the most seats, but Stanley Baldwin became PM.
- Wall Street Crash which started the 12 year Great Depression.
- General Election in which the Labour Party won most seats. Ramsay MacDonald became PM.
- Paul Galvin invented the car radio.
- Best selling novels included *The Sound and the Fury* by William Faulkner, *The Great Gatsby* by F Scott Fitzgerald and *A Farewell to Arms* by Ernest Hemingway.

1930
- Frank Whittle registered the patent for his turbo jet engine.
- Infant mortality: 63 deaths per 1,000 births.
- Arthur Ransome published the first of the twelve 'Swallows and Amazons' books.

Bing Crosby made his first record as a solo vocalist with the Gus Arnheim orchestra, his new type of singing voice gradually replaced the typical tenor of the 1920s.

J B Priestley published *Angel Pavement*.

1931

UK population reached 46 million.

National government formed with Labour, Conservative and Liberal MPs under Ramsay MacDonald.

Unemployment reached 2·67 million.

Gracie Fields made her first film *Sally in Our Alley* which included her most famous song 'Sally'.

1932

Gerhard Domagiz led the research team which developed Prontosil, the first commercially available anti-bacterial antibiotic.

Publication of *Brave New World* by Aldous Huxley.

W E Johns created the character 'Biggles' who was a pilot and adventurer. The first collection of stories was published as *The Camels are Coming*. W E Johns continued writing Biggles stories until his death in 1968.

1933

Adolf Hitler became Chancellor of Germany.

UK unemployment reached 2·97 million.

Popular films included *I'm No Angel* (Paramount), *Dinner at Eight* (MGM) and *42nd Street* (Warner Bros).

Publication of *Tender is the Night* by F Scott Fitzgerald and *Tropic of Cancer* by Henry Miller.

Dinky Toy cars came onto the market. They were originally known as 'Modelled Miniatures' but became Dinky Toys in 1934.

1934

Gresford colliery disaster in which 266 miners and rescuers lost their lives.

Road Traffic Act introduced compulsory testing for all drivers and a speed limit of 30 miles per hour was introduced on roads in built-up areas.

No speed limit applied on other roads.
Percy Shaw invented 'cat's eyes' for use as road reflectors.
Charles Darrow invented the popular board game 'Monopoly'.
Robert Graves published *I, Claudius* and James Hilton published *Goodbye Mr Chips*.

1935

Conservatives won General Election with Stanley Baldwin becoming Prime Minister.
Average family size included 2·4 children.
The first canned beer made.
Ramblers Association founded.
Allen Lane founded Penguin Books.
The film *Becky Sharp* was released: the first feature film made in full colour.
Most popular novels published include *Little House on the Prairie* by Laura Ingalls Wilder and *Tortilla Flat* by John Steinbeck.

1936

Constitutional crisis arising from abdication of King Edward VIII.
Start of the Spanish Civil War. 4,000 British people volunteered during the war to fight for the Republican cause.
Billy Butlin opened his first holiday camp at Skegness.
Giles Gilbert Scott produced a refinement (K6) of earlier telephone box designs which then became the established model for public telephone call boxes for the rest of the century.
The first 'Rupert Bear Annual' was published.

1937

Coronation of King George VI.
Neville Chamberlain succeeded Stanley Baldwin as leader of the Conservative Party.
Introduction of the 999 emergency telephone number.
Fred Perry turned professional after winning Wimbledon in 1934, 1935 and 1936.
Publication of *The Hobbit* by J R R Tolkien.

TIMELINE OF BRITISH SOCIAL HISTORY: 1925–1950

Launch of the comic *The Dandy* featuring Desperate Dan.

Hit songs included Count Basie's 'One O'Clock Jump' and Benny Goodman's 'Sing, Sing, Sing'.

1938

Neville Chamberlain signed the Munich Agreement with Adolf Hitler and gave his 'peace for our time' speech.

Production of the Spitfire (K9787) began at Woolston, Southampton.

Sales began in the UK of drum-type tumbler dryers based on a design by American J Ross Moore. The early model was called the 'June Day'.

Release of Walt Disney's film *Snow White and the Seven Dwarfs:* the first animated feature film produced in America.

Ball point pen invented by Ladislo Biro.

Publication of Daphne du Maurier's novel *Rebecca*.

First appearance of 'Superman' in Action Comics.

Launch of the comic *The Beano*.

1939

Outbreak of Second World War.

Evacuation of three million people, mainly children from towns and cities. Children were supervised by 100,000 teachers.

Suspension of television services for duration of the war.

Release of classic American films *Gone with the Wind* and *The Wizard of Oz*.

Launch of popular radio programme *ITMA,* featuring Tommy Handley, which ran to 1949.

Glen Miller and his orchestra recorded the hit 'Moonlight Serenade'.

1940

Winston Churchill succeeded Neville Chamberlain as PM, declaring 'I have nothing to offer you but blood, toil, tears and sweat'.

Evacuation of 300,000 British and French troops from Dunkirk (May).

Battle of Britain in which the RAF claimed victory over the Luftwaffe and deterred Hitler from invading this country (September).

The Blitz: the sustained German strategic bombing of British cities in 1940/41 which destroyed more than one million homes and killed more than 40,000 civilians.

Food rationing introduced.

HMT *Lancastria* bombed in St Nazaire whilst evacuating British troops and nationals. 4,000 people lost their lives: the largest single UK loss in the war.

1941

Japanese surprise attack on American fleet in Pearl Harbour, which led to US entry into Second World War.

Population reached 48·2 million.

Frank Whittle's jet flew for the first time.

Aerosol spray can invented by Lyle David Goodloe and W N Sullivan.

Noel Coward's play *Blithe Spirit* opened in West End.

Glen Miller recorded 'Chattanooga Choo Choo'.

First broadcast of *Worker's Playtime*, a BBC programme designed to boost morale. It was broadcast from a factory canteen 'somewhere in Britain'. The programme ran until 1964.

1942

General Montgomery's army in North Africa won the battle of El Alamein and Rommel started his retreat.

640,000 women in the armed forces.

Glen Miller recorded 'Don't Sit Under the Apple Tree' and 'I've Got a Gal in Kalamazoo'.

Enid Blyton published *Five on a Treasure Island;* the first in a series of 21.

Release of Walt Disney's classic animated film *Bambi*.

1943

90% of single women and 80% of married women working in factories, on the land or in armed forces. 80,000 women in the Land Army earned £1·85 for a minimum 50 hour week.

Noel Coward was awarded Academy Honorary Award for his naval film drama *In Which We Serve*.

Publication of *The Little Prince* by Antoine de Saint Exupery.

1944

D-Day. US and British troops landed on the beaches of Normandy.

Paris liberated.

Battle of the Bulge: the last German offensive.

Rab Butler introduced his Education Act which created a tripartite system of secondary education with secondary modern, technical and grammar schools. Entry was determined by the eleven plus examination.

Road fatalities: four per 1,000 vehicles.

1945

Victory in Europe for Allies.

Atomic bombs dropped on Hiroshima and Nagasaki.

Landslide victory for Labour Party in General Election. Clement Attlee became PM.

Publication of *Animal Farm* by George Orwell.

Hit songs included 'Sentimental Journey' sung by Les Brown and Doris Day and 'Rum and Coca Cola' sung by the Andrews Sisters.

1946

Cinema audiences peaked at 1,640 million. Popular films were *The Best Years of Our Lives* (William Wyler), *The Big Sleep* (Howard Hawks) and *Brief Encounter* (David Lean).

Alan Turing presented a paper with the first detailed design of a stored programme computer. He is regarded as the father of computer science.

Introduction of the Family Allowance, which was worth five shillings per child per week. This was changed to 'Child Benefit' in 1977.

Resumption of television services coincided with introduction of television licence.

Children's Hour: television's first programme for children. Enter 'Muffin the Mule' with Annette Mills.

First broadcast of *Womans Hour* and *Housewives Choice*.

First broadcast of *Dick Barton Special Agent*. The series ran until 1951 and had a peak audience of 15 million listeners. The memorable signature tune was 'Devil's Gallop' by Charles Williams.

First broadcast of BBC radio programme *Have a Go* compered by Wilfred Pickles with the catch phrases 'Are you courting?' and 'What's on the table Mabel?' The programme ran until 1967

Publication of Dr Benjamin Spock's influential *The Common Sense Book of Baby and Child Care.*

Manufacture of Dinky Toys resumed with the first post-war model being a jeep.

1947

School leaving age was raised to 15.

10 self-service shops in UK.

West End performance of Rodgers and Hammerstein musical *Oklahoma.*

Hits included 'Prisoner of Love' (Perry Como), 'Five Minutes More' (Frank Sinatra) and 'Open the Door, Richard' (originally recorded by saxophonist Jackie McVea).

1948

Introduction of the National Health Service by Minister of Health Aneurin Bevin.

The Empire Windrush docked in Tilbury bringing hundreds of men from the West Indies. This was the start of mass immigration into the UK.

First studies of smoking habits: 82% of men smoked some form of tobacco, 41% of women were smokers.

Columbia records started to market the 33 ⅓ rotations per minute long playing (LP) record.

Mrs Dale's Diary, the first radio soap, began a long series of 15 minute programmes.

1949

BBC television service started to spread outside London.

The first UK launderette opened in Queensway, London.

Publication of *1984* by George Orwell.

Popular songs included Vaughn Monroe 'Riders in the Sky', Gene Autry 'Rudolph the Red-Nosed Reindeer' and Frankie Lane 'Mule Train'.

1950

Korean War began: 1,078 British servicemen were killed and 1,060 were either missing or taken prisoner.

Richard Doll published research in BMJ showing a close link between smoking and lung cancer.

Vladimir Raitz pioneered the first mass package holidays with charter flights between Gatwick and Corsica.

First publication of the 'Chronicles of Narnia' series by C S Lewis.

Andy Pandy first appeared on children's television.

Listen with Mother began: a long-running radio series for children under five.

MAUREEN WILDASH

*Maureen Wildash (née Geoghegan)
was born in Highgate, London, in May 1930*

I was born in Highgate, but due to family traumas much of my childhood was spent, with my elder sister Joan, in a convent, initially in Hendon and then in Cirencester. One of my earliest memories is a Sister running down the corridors shouting, 'The war is ended!' This was the Spanish Civil War, which as children we knew nothing about.

An early memory is being taken ill one night with a sore throat and being rushed to Charing Cross Hospital. I had diphtheria and remember a man carrying me on what I thought was a lorry, and later put on a bed when big needles were put in my thighs, I thought that I would never walk again it hurt so much. I was in hospital for eleven weeks and was frightened the whole time. My mother was allowed to peep at me through the curtains and when I saw her I'd scream some more. I had my fifth birthday there and I recall a pink doll, which I had to leave behind.

The Sisters, who belonged to a German Order, had purchased a large mansion in Cirencester as a Rest Home in 1938. This was Chesterton House and it had been the last home of the White Rajah of Sarawak. Our mother took us there for a month's holiday in August 1939 but we never returned to London. One day a Sister came into our bedroom and told us that the War had started. I screamed and hid under the bedclothes expecting soldiers with swords to rush in, my knowledge of war being gained from picture books.

We remained in Cirencester throughout the war. All our friends, the London boarders, came down with trunks full of toys. Day scholars

Maureen (right) poses with her sister Joan in her grandmother's garden on the occasion of her first Holy Communion (1938).

appeared and we were astonished at their Gloucestershire accents. London voices were all we knew. We went for walks in crocodile lines with a Sister front and back to make sure we behaved ourselves, but it was all so different from London. Buses were labelled with where they were coming from and not their destination to confuse the enemy. This amused even our young minds.

Soldiers and airmen in uniform were everywhere and it was rare to see a young man not in uniform. One of the worst aspects on a day-to-day basis was the blackout. We had to have a torch if we went out at night and point it at the ground to see where we were stepping. Everyone was issued with a gas mask in a cardboard box with a handle. We were not allowed to go out without it. As the war went on we were given leather cases as presents as the cardboard boxes soon fell to pieces. We had to practise using them but I could not breathe with it on. I remember thinking that I could never actually be able to wear mine if the occasion arose. 'Don't forget your mask!' was called out whenever we went out. We were safe in the country but the Blitz was going on in London and terrible things were happening. An uncle and aunt were bombed in London and lost everything. They came and stayed with us in Gloucestershire to recover. Unfortunately my parents had all their possessions stored in their loft and therefore lost everything.

Air raids came near us later on. The German bombers used to fly overhead night after night on their way to Coventry, Bristol and other strategic targets. We would hear the sirens night after night, a dreadful sound. Each one of us had a bedroll at the foot of our beds. When the siren sounded we all had to get up, take our bedroll and go downstairs to our allotted places. I was in the youngest set and our place was on the shelves in the wine cellars. We tried to go back to sleep and when the 'all-clear' sounded we tottered back to bed again. I can still see the Sisters running along the corridors clanging a bell and there was always a feeling of panic.

Food rationing was something we just had to put up with. And we certainly didn't get much to eat beyond the basics. It must have been awful to be a housewife. Everyone had a ration book and I remember a few details from when I grew older and went home for weekends and holidays from 1944 onwards. The weekly ration of butter and margarine was two ounces; one shilling and two pence worth of meat each week some of which as corned beef and one jar of jam or marmalade per month. Fresh eggs were rare and so mainly we had dried eggs, a yellow powder, which tasted horrible but we ate with relish because we were so hungry. We did not have a single orange or banana during the entire war. I well remember the first bananas coming in late 1945 and the smaller children did not know what they were and some of us older ones had to show them how to peel them. Sweets and chocolates were a rarity and I seem to remember we were allowed two ounces per week. Clothes were also rationed and we had clothes coupons. Poor people sold their coupons. My mother was a dressmaker among other things and was brilliant at converting old garments into new ones. I remember her making a coat from a blanket and dyeing it green. I never had new clothes and always wore my sister's 'cast-offs'. We did not worry too much as very few of our friends were even remotely smart.

As well as running the boarding house and her family my mother also had to do 'war work'. She had applied to the Air Ministry but was rejected on account of her maiden name, which was German, Klefisch.

She was therefore directed to work in a Munitions factory where she sometimes had to work during the night shift. I remember so well waving her off at bedtime, wearing her turban which all the women wore to prevent accidents. We used to tease her about her milling and grinding and her efforts to obtain bonuses. Watching out for air raids from the rooftops was another duty she carried out. Considering that she had never previously worked in her life before the war this was a remarkable achievement.

The American servicemen were a constant factor in our lives as their camp was just up our road. In the context of school they brought fun into our lives, shouting into the classrooms when they marched past and even following the crocodile walks to town. The Sisters were very put out! The girls from the Air Ministry had GI's chasing them and often my mother would sort them out when they made dates with more than one and the extra suitor duly arrived on our doorstep. The Americans were very generous to us with goodies and I remember an eight pound tin of marmalade. One day we heard a huge rumbling sound and the entire American camp was on the move. All the covered wagons were full of soldiers waving and calling 'good-bye'. We felt so sad. This was D Day and for sure many of those boys never returned.

Months later we became aware of the Prisoner of War (POW) camps nearby. We were studying German and we liked to talk to these boys through the barbed wire. They were mostly under twenty. We did not know their history but felt sad for them. However, in Cirencester Park there was another POW camp and we could see that the prisoners were in a different category, partly because they were heavily guarded. They were members of the SS and we felt chilled.

VE Day May 1945. Oh! What a day! I was allowed to go home as there were no lessons. Everyone was happy and smiling. The town was filled with soldiers and airmen. At home we all mixed up with the neighbours. In the evening we put the piano in the bay window, someone played and everyone danced in the street. The most marvellous thing was that all the lights were on! No blackout! My sister and I went into the town, which was so crowded. I got my first kiss from an airman! We hardly slept that night; to think that there was no more war!

As the weeks went by and we saw the newsreels at the cinema, and saw the pictures in the newspapers our joy was diminished. We heard about the terrible things the Jews had suffered and the millions of displaced persons. I have never forgotten the films of Auschwitz and Belsen and to think that we had been living our lives during such happenings. In contrast there were great family celebrations when one of my cousins, who had been captured at Dunkirk, came home.

I left school one year after the war ended and took a job as a telephone 'Hello' girl. Two years later I obtained a job as a bank clerk in London. At my interview with the manager, aged sixteen, he asked me if I was thrifty. I did not even know what the word meant but I said, 'Yes!'

City girls! Maureen and Joan in London when Maureen was working as a bank clerk (1948).

Maureen Wildash left school at sixteen and worked in a number of clerical jobs, including being the first female clerk in the New Zealand Bank in London. After two years she returned to Gloucestershire to help her parents where she met her first husband, Alan. Maureen has a daughter, Gillian and three sons, Michael, Nicholas and Andrew. 'All I ever wanted was a home of my own and a family.' Maureen has lived for most of her adult life in Cornwall and Devon.

JEAN RICHARDSON

Jean Richardson (née Purvis) was born in Blyth, Northumberland, in October 1931.

I was born in Blyth, a seaport town in Northumberland, in 1931. Blyth was a busy town. It had a big shipyard, several coal mines and the harbour was always full of ships coming and going. Coal was shipped all over the country and there was plenty of work for teamers and trimmers who worked in the ships' holds. They were well paid and much sought-after jobs.

My father was a bus driver and my mother was always at home for my brother, Bobby, and me. I was nearly five years older than Bobby. I had a happy childhood. I can remember the day I started school and felt very grown up. My mother took me and I can remember her saying she would be back to collect me at dinner time. In those days there were no school dinners but mam always had a hot meal ready for us at midday. The school was just at the top of our street so I was soon going up and down to school on my own. My mother was a great knitter and all of my school jumpers and skirts were knitted by her. I can remember one of my teachers asking me who knitted my clothes and when I told her mam did, she said I was a very lucky girl.

I was at junior school when war was declared in 1939. I can remember sitting by the wireless with mam and dad and Bobby listening to Mr Neville Chamberlain and when he said we were at war with Germany my mam just cried and cried. When I asked dad why she was crying he said he would probably have to go away and join the army so that he could look after us all. We lived in an upstairs flat in a street of terraced houses. I can remember going downstairs with mam and

Bobby where all the neighbours had gathered together and everyone was talking about what was going to happen. Suddenly the piercing air raid siren sounded. No one knew what to do, so everyone ran into their own houses. Mrs Tait, who lived in the flat below us, asked us to come and shelter in her house, so we all crowded into the cupboard under her stairs, and there we sat until the 'all clear' sounded. However, it had been a false alarm!

Dad wasn't called up to join the army as he had a reserved occupation. We didn't know that at first, but mam thought she had better find a job just in case he went away. When she heard that Blyth shipyard was recruiting women she was one of the first ones there and she stayed at the shipyard until the war ended. My grandma lived in the same street as us and she came to help look after Bobby and I when mam was at work. We always thought of grandma being very old. She wore long black skirts and blouses and she always had a big black shawl over her shoulders. She can only have been in her fifties.

Dad joined the Home Guard, along with most of his bus driver friends. My teacher at junior school was Mr George Sanderson, who had been a soldier in the First World War, and he was put in charge of the United Bus Company Home Guard Unit. I am not sure what rank he was but he was an officer and he wore a much smarter uniform than dad and his friends. Mr Sanderson used to give me notices to give to my dad and I felt so important taking these home. I felt I was doing work for the war effort.

We didn't have a garden so we couldn't have an Anderson Shelter but my Aunt Madge and Uncle Billy had an Anderson shelter in their garden so when the siren sounded we used to run over to their house about half a mile away, and scramble down into their shelter. It was awful when the siren went off during the night and we had to run over to Chestnut Avenue in the dark. We eventually had a shelter in our street so then we just had to run downstairs. The shelters were cold damp places but the wives made them as comfortable as possible.

Blyth didn't suffer too much in the air raids. I can remember hearing the 'Bang!' when a bomb was dropped on the station yard. It was just a few streets away from us and we could hear all the windows in our houses being shattered. Only one person was killed that night.

He was working in the signal box at the station which took a direct hit. Another bomb was dropped near the docks but, fortunately, there were no casualties.

Going to school meant we had to take a piece of equipment with us, our gas masks. We had regular 'try outs' at school and one day two ARP wardens came and told us what we had to do if there was a gas attack. They showed us the correct way to wear our masks, then we had to go singly into a room wearing our gas masks where there actually was some gas. It couldn't have been very much, but if we smelt gas we had to go out and the wardens would check our masks and if they thought they were faulty then they would give us a new one. I can remember some boys having a fight in the school yard and they were hitting each other over the head with their gas mask cases, gas masks being inside them of course!

The Air Raid Wardens came into their own when there was an air raid. If there was a chink of light coming from anyone's house they would bang on their door and yell, 'Put that light out there!' In our front room we didn't have blackout curtains at first and if one of us pressed the wrong switch and the front room light went on … chaos! As the war went on, people were fined if they showed a light, particularly if they had had a warning. It wasn't long before our front room had its blackout blinds.

Everyone carried on as normal during the war. I still went to Brownies and later to Girl Guides. My best friend was Hazel and we went everywhere together. We still think of each other as best friends, seventy years on, even though we don't see each other very often. Nobody went on holiday during the war but we did go camping with our Girl Guides. These camps were the highlight of our year. We didn't go far away, the furthest would be about thirty miles, but there was such excitement as we boarded the bus, being waved off by our parents. We slept in big bell tents, eight or ten of us lying side by side in our sleeping bags. The tents were put up for us the day before by a working party of Guide leaders who also dug latrines and prepared the cooking area. When we arrived at camp we were split up into patrols and Hazel and I always managed to get into the same patrol even though we were told we had to mix with Guides from other companies. There would be a system for mixing us but we managed to figure out the system and made sure we were together. Each patrol took a turn to cook, collect water from the river, gather wood for the campfire, general fatigues and cleaning the dixies (big cooking pots). We were kept busy all day and were always ready for our meals which we ate with great gusto and we queued for seconds if there was anything left. We loved our evening camp fires, singing our favourite songs and sipping our cocoa. The latrines were in the next field and if you needed to go during the night, it was quite a trek struggling out of our sleeping bags and climbing over everyone to get out of the tent and then dashing across the field in the dark.

We went to the pictures often. There were three cinemas in our town and they changed their programmes twice a week. There were two showings, six o'clock and eight o'clock in the evening and you always had to queue to get in. Sometimes the film would be interrupted by a newsflash saying 'The siren has sounded. Please leave the cinema in an orderly fashion.' At first, everyone responded, but then folk became very blasé and just stayed watching the film until we heard a bomb blast and then everyone hurriedly left and went to the nearest shelter. Another notice might read 'Will the crew of HMS —— please return to their ship immediately'. Blyth was a submarine base during the war so there were always lots of sailors in the town and when the return to ship notice was shown, several men would get up from their seats and hurry back to their ship.

Blyth has lovely beaches but of course we couldn't go there or the harbour during the war. The entrances were guarded by armed soldiers and if you got too close, they would shout, 'Halt! Who goes there?'

You had to reply 'Friend,' then explain what you were doing there.

There were big gun emplacements all along the sand dunes and search lights too. When there was an air raid on, it was fascinating watching the enemy planes being caught in the searchlight. There were air bases a few miles out of town and barrage balloon stations, so there were plenty of army, navy and airforce men and women around. Part of our church hall was turned into a NAAFI and ladies from our church helped there. Hazel and I were too young to help but we usually found an excuse to go to the hall and depending which ladies were on duty, we might just be able to buy a bar of chocolate. Our sweet ration didn't go very far, three ounces a week, so an extra bar of chocolate without coupons was a real bonus.

We had some bad winters during the 1940s. Lots of snow and ice during the war years but I don't remember the traffic coming to a real stand still. The buses always managed to keep going and of course there weren't many cars on the road as petrol was strictly rationed. It wasn't easy for the bus drivers during the blackout as their headlights were covered and only slits of light could be seen. Everyone carried a torch and none of these had very bright beams. We really needed our torches on dark winters nights with no street light to guide us, but I don't remember any accidents and crime was non-existent. When the ice and snow began to thaw, we had to carefully walk down the middle of the road as it was too dangerous to walk on the pavements due to the deep snow falling from the rooftops. I don't ever remember our schools being closed due to the weather and we always managed to have our Brownie and Girl Guide and youth club meetings and of course church and Sunday school.

We spent a lot of time queuing. Most goods were in short supply. We all had our ration cards and food rationing meant that we all had a few ounces each of butter, margarine, sugar, cheese, meat, bread, eggs and other necessities. We had a sweet ration, it was twelve ounces a month, but there wasn't a great selection of sweets to choose from. Cigarettes weren't rationed but they were always in short supply. A lot of people smoked and if a shop had a delivery of cigarettes, word would spread like wildfire and a huge queue would form in just a few minutes. Likewise with sweets. If a delivery van was seen at a shop, then there was queue before the van left and the shop very quickly sold out of their delivery, particularly if it was chocolate. The queues were mostly friendly and good-hearted. Everyone chatted and exchanged stories whilst waiting to be served and if the shop sold out of whatever they were selling before it was our turn to be served, then there were groans of disappointment but we just moved on to another queue at another shop.

One day at school, we were told to put on our coats, hats, scarves and gloves and assemble in the school yard. Then our Headmaster told us we were going to walk into Blyth town centre and we had to walk in twos in a very orderly fashion. He didn't tell us why we were going, but we were all excited at this unexpected change in our school routine. As we walked with our teachers into town, we were aware of lots of people following us and there was a buzz of excitement in the air. Then when we arrived near the railway station we stood in an orderly line and we were told why we were there. King George VI and Queen Elizabeth were on their way to Blyth Ship Yard and the Queen was going to launch a ship. What excitement! We were actually going to see our King and Queen in person and not just on the Movietone News at the cinema. Their car came slowly into view and we all screamed and cheered. The Queen was wearing blue and the King was in his naval uniform. They both smiled and waved at us and we were all so thrilled.

I passed the grading exam when I was eleven and went to grammar school. There was a school uniform but when mam and I went to Soulsbys, the shop which sold our uniforms, we were told they could no longer get maroon blazers, and our hats and school badges were not being made as the textile factories were making uniforms for our armed forces. We then wore navy blazers and if we were lucky, we were given a badge from an old blazer which had worn out. We also wore white shirts and navy skirts or trousers for the boys. The uniform included navy-blue caps for boys and navy-blue berets for girls. The grammar school was about two miles from where I lived. One Christmas I was given a BSA bicycle, my pride and joy, and I cycled to school every day. We had school dinners which were always very good in spite of rationing and they cost six pence a day. There were always two sittings so the time of our dinner hour depended on which sitting we had to attend.

Our teachers were mainly ladies and one or two older gentlemen. All the young male teachers were called up into the armed forces. On the whole I enjoyed school and made lifelong friends there. Now seventy years on, four of us still occasionally get together and we regularly phone each other. One day Miss Crisp, our French teacher, introduced us to a young man who had escaped from France which was now occupied by Germany. He was a member of Amis des Voluntaires Françaises, part of the French Resistance Movement.

He had us all enthralled by his stories and asked us if we would like to become friends of the French Volunteers, so most of us joined the AVF. He gave us all an AVF badge, which we could wear on our blazers. We weren't allowed to wear any jewellery when we were in uniform, apart from a watch, so our AVF badge was very prominent. We didn't do very much for the movement, apart from buying their regular newspaper, but I don't remember doing anything exciting.

We were always interested in war news and had regular discussions at school. The radio news was a 'must' to listen to and when we went to the pictures the Movietone News was always shown before the feature film and kept us up to date with the war effort. I well remember the excitement when the war turned in our favour in the Middle East and we had Rommel and his forces on the run. There was such excitement in the cinema and everyone was on their feet clapping and cheering. Some of our friends were telegram boys who delivered telegrams on their bicycles. One horrible job was delivering a telegram telling wives and mothers that their husband or son was missing in action, presumed killed. A horrible time for everyone.

When I was fourteen, I was aware that one of the choir boys in church was looking at me. He was eighteen, a lot older than me, so I took no notice of him. Then one day he smiled at me and said, 'Hello.' I was a bit taken aback but smiled and said, 'Hello' as well. That was how I met Jim Richardson who became my first, and only boyfriend.

The day the war ended was a day of sheer joy. Hazel and I went to Blyth market place where there was singing and dancing all night and everyone was so happy. We fully expected everyone to take down their blackout blinds straight away but no-one did. I think everyone was in a

Jim and Jean with their bikes (1948).

state of disbelief! And we expected the sweet shops to be full and that we wouldn't need our ration cards to buy our sweets, but rationing was to last for a few more years.

Hazel and I moved up from Girl Guides to join a company of Sea Rangers, which was just about to begin. We loved being part of SRS (Sea Ranger Ship) Trevelyan. The war was over and the riverside and beaches were open to the public again and our Sea Ranger meeting place was a recently vacated hut in Blyth harbour. There were twenty-four of us girls and we were put into two groups, port and starboard. We had a real ship's bell, which was rung when we first assembled and as we left. We were thrilled when we were able to get our own ship, which was an old rowing boat. I don't know where it came from but it gave us all endless pleasure. We took great pride in painting her and when we painted *SRS Trevelyan* on the bows we were all as pleased as punch. She was launched in Blyth harbour. I thought we all could fit into her but I'm not sure now, twenty-four excited girls in a rowing boat sounds a bit overwhelming! We all took turns at the oars. Hazel was very good but I never quite managed the rhythm and always managed to make a big splash when everyone got soaked. We all had to learn tying knots and various seamanship skills, and we had to learn to swim. Hazel and I spent hours in our cold North Sea trying to swim but we eventually made it. We had to swim two lengths in a swimming pool before we could proudly announce that we were swimmers. We loved wearing our Sea Ranger uniforms. Some ex-WRNS gave us their navy hats and we wore

Jean with her friend Hazel in London for the Ranger Rally (1948).

them with great pride knowing they had been worn 'in action.'

A big highlight was when some of our crew were able to join a Ranger Rally at the Albert Hall in London in 1948. What excitement! None of us had been to London before so this was a great adventure. We went by train overnight, not in a sleeper so we chatted for most of the night. We were met by some London Rangers who took us to a church hall near Kings Cross station where there were camp beds and blankets awaiting us and a hot meal. Then we freshened up and were off by underground railway to the Albert Hall. What a moving experience this was. We were welcomed by Lady Baden-Powell, Chief Guide of the World and wife of Lord Baden-Powell who founded the Boy Scout movement. She was lovely and when she finished addressing us, a packed Albert Hall rose as one to cheer and clap her. I don't remember much about the rest of the meeting apart from the parade of flags from every county in the UK and one or two from Europe. A tremendous cheer went up when a flag from Germany was paraded. Most of us were in tears and the Ranger carrying the German flag was overwhelmed by her reception. Next day was another spectacular day. We all assembled outside a large stadium, I can't remember which one, and then we all paraded into the stadium, county by county, where Princess Margaret was taking the salute. We were so very, very proud. Then it was over! Back to Kings Cross and the overnight train to Newcastle.

Jean married Jim Richardson in 1952 and they immediately sailed out to South Africa where they spent eighteen very happy years. Initially they worked in a mission school in Zululand and later at a private boys school in Johannesburg. They then moved to Swaziland where Jim built Waterford School, a multi-racial school, where Jean was the first matron. They raised their family of five children in Africa: Andrew, Peter, David, Christine and Virginia. On their return to England in 1970 they worked at an approved school near Newcastle teaching young delinquent boys.

'Sadly Jim died in 2008, but I have a lifetime of wonderful memories and a wonderful family too.'

GILL HOLT

Gill Holt (née Smith) was born in Oxford in October 1933

I was six years old when the Second World War started, but I knew nothing about it and just accepted that my father had disappeared. He was twenty-five years old and joined the Royal Army Medical Corps for the duration of the war. I only saw him once in the six years of the war, when he came home on leave to where my mother and I were living with her mother and father in a village outside Oxford. I shared a bedroom with my mother and I had to move out while he was there. I think I was about eight years old. When I came home from the village school the day after he arrived I found my mother's clothes, jewellery and bottles of scent strewn on the front lawn. He had gone. Nobody said anything but I worked out that he must have thrown my mother's things out of the window when they had a row. My mother had been a very attractive twenty-five-year-old when the war started and easily obtained several jobs in factories and shops. For the first time, like so many other wives with husbands in the war, she had her own money to

Gill aged two and a half in her gran's garden in Kennington, near Oxford (1936). 'I remember the roses.'

spend on having a good time. I remember my gran telling her to enjoy herself while she had the chance. Some of my contemporaries at school also had fathers in the Services and their mothers, like mine, had men friends. There were plenty of uniformed officers stationed nearby, and also the Americans at the airbases. I don't think my mother went out with any of these but plenty of local girls did, and I was well aware that that when a sixteen-year-old girl became pregnant the father was probably an American. These babies were often brought up by their grandmothers and thought their mothers were their sisters. As children we knew all about the sex that went on between the local teenage girls and the Americans because we saw them in the fields together. Several of us used to line up on the wall of a house on the way home from school to watch a girl in the front room with her boyfriend. I don't think that our village was a hotbed of sexual shenanigans, any more than any other districts I imagine. When we saw a 'dirty old man' open his raincoat and expose himself, we just laughed and continued with our childish games.

My five years at the village school, before I went to grammar school, were blissful. Yes, there were unpleasant times, but we took them in our stride: being chased by boys who put snakes down our necks, being caned by the teacher when I willed myself not to flinch, being rapped across the knuckle with a ruler for not getting my long division sums right, going to the outside toilet across the playground where the boys would tease us. Other unpleasant experiences included the 'snot and bogey' suet roll, which appeared regularly in school dinners and the tepid bottles of milk which the teacher put beside the fire to warm up for us. Yuk! The pleasant things were games in the playground, hiding under coats, playing tag,

A school photo of Gill age six and a half. 'Mum made the dress with orange flowers and a Peter Pan collar.'

running round the school, listening to stories, reading books, being ink monitor and filling the ink wells, and being allowed to tidy the stationery cupboard.

Walking home from school was always an adventure. Which way to go? Walking home in winter through thick fog so you couldn't see where you were going was scary. Jumping on people's hedges to bounce off and be shouted at was great fun and I am still tempted to do it today, at the age of seventy-six, when I pass a nice hedge. There were happy afternoons bouncing a ball against someone's garage door, climbing up onto their sheds or scrumping their apples. The only time my mother chastised me was when I scrumped in next door's garden. Our neighbour must have told her. Most of the time my mother never knew what I was doing because she was out at work.

The joy of long summer holidays seemed endless. Occasionally we would go down to the railway line and place halfpennies on the track for trains to run over and turn them into pennies. Sometimes we would spend days up in the woods where men could be shooting. We climbed trees, scrambled over the dump and gravel pit or ran down to the river to get at the yellow water lilies floating on the surface with their slimy stems going down into the water. I fell in once but fortunately my friend's older sister was there and hauled me out. We could swim out to the girder of the iron railway bridge across the river. The older boys showed off by diving into the river from the top of one of the arches. Once, three of us girls stole a boat and paddled it down the river until it started leaking when we just managed to get it ashore, where we left it and struggled through the undergrowth to get home. We loved to go into the farmer's fields and be chased by him and his white bull terrier. The joy at clambering over the fence before he reached us was wonderful. We laughed when we saw him brandishing his stick. We ate the new shoots of the hawthorn and called it 'bread and cheese'. We knew where to find the earliest blackberries and hazel nuts and splashed across the meadows by the Thames to find the rare 'snake's heads' (fritillaries). We played rounders in our village street and stayed out till dark until we were scared by the bats. I had a wonderful carefree childhood.

Home for me was the place where I ate the meals that my gran prepared for me and where my gramp cleaned my muddy shoes. One of the great pleasures of home was reading a book, either in the apple tree or under the fir tree on the dry sweet-smelling ground covered with pine needles. Sometimes I imagined that I could see fairies on the purple irises. I liked to watch my gramp digging in the garden and sometimes I would brave the prickles of the gooseberry bush to pick gooseberries that my gran would make into a pie. I hardly ever saw my mother because she was either at work or out dancing or in the pub.

The end of my childhood coincided with the end of the war in 1945 when I was twelve years old. My parents were getting divorced and I was asked whom I wanted to live with. Naturally I said my mother. We children had got so used to the grown-ups saying 'when the war is over' that we thought that something marvellous was going to happen but in the event it was a bit of a let down. VE Day came and went and nothing wonderful happened. The first bananas that I ever tasted were a great disappointment.

I passed the eleven plus examination and went to a grammar school. After a village school full of working class country kids it was strange to hear girls with posh voices. The year I started the school had changed from a fee-paying school to a state grammar school. The only posh voices I had heard in my village were from the two girls who lived in the 'big house'. One day when they got off the bus that took them to a private school in Oxford the younger girl wanted to stop and talk to us but her elder sister remonstrated with her 'Remember what mother said. You ought not to talk to the common village children'. That was my second experience of class consciousness and set my attitudes for life. The first experience had been when I was six. My grandfather was the groundsman of an Oxford College sports ground and one sports day there was a race for the children of the undergraduates' families. I had been told that the prize was a doll's pram which I coveted above all else. I would never have had one given to me, too expensive for a groundsman's granddaughter. Anyway I entered the race and won, but I was not given the doll's pram. At six years old I could not understand this decision, which was based on social class, but I do now.

Gill Holt left school at the age of fifteen without any qualifications and worked in a variety of jobs where she was paid about a pound per week.

She married at eighteen and raised a family of four children. In her late twenties she returned to her lost education, and eventually obtained the qualifications to enter Teacher Training College where she graduated at the age of thirty-nine and taught English for eighteen years.

'My mother's marriage broke up during the war when women found they could be independent and so did mine for the same reason when I decided to further my education.'

GREN GASKELL
Gren Gaskell was born in Bulwell, Nottingham, in July 1936

The man strode toward me holding something in a cloth bag and pushed me towards a cage containing a ferret. He opened a little door and shook the contents of the bag in to where the animal waited and held me to watch while the ferret thrashed about killing the live sparrows, which fluttered in panic around the confined space. Blood was splattering the box as I was forced to see the feathers and flesh torn from the birds and looked up to the face of the man whose distorted features conveyed his perverted enjoyment. I was six or seven years old at the time.

This incident burned into my mind and was part of my introduction to the man who was to be my step-father. He was a miner in his forties and had never been married. His main interests were running greyhounds, rabbiting with ferrets and cock fighting. Sometimes he would know someone with 'permission', this meant he could catch game without breaking the law, but mostly he was poaching. There was very little communication between us over the next forty years but I asked him before he died what was the best part of his life and he said it was the strike in 1926. It had been a hot summer and he had been out with the dogs every day.

Throughout my childhood he had an urge to teach me the ways of his cruelty. Perhaps this was because he knew how revolted I was by the suffering he caused. Perhaps he genuinely wanted to pass on his knowledge of the complicated tortures he had learned or devised himself. There were plenty of opportunities for him to practise. People from the neighbourhood would bring unwanted kittens and puppies for him to dispose of, totally unaware of their fate. He certainly despised me for being a softy. 'You are no bloody good and you never will be as long as you've got an 'ole in your arse,' he told me over and over again. I believed it for much of my life. He knocked us about, my brothers, sisters and mam as well.

My older siblings left home as quickly as they could following the re-marriage of our mother and I learned recently that one brother ran away to London when the authorities were evacuating people from the capital to escape the Blitz. He refused to be sent home and worked in Lyon's Corner House rather than live in the unhappy household where I was trapped.

We were never to be a normal family. Dad was killed at Bestwood Colliery leaving six small children and a widow whose income was one pound five shillings a week. The first call on this sum was the rent because, rightly or wrongly, mam had a dread of us all ending up in the workhouse. She had a fear of authority so we were left to cope in a desperate situation and, for reasons difficult to understand, my mam found it impossible to accept the little help she was offered.

When I was older I asked if these stories relayed from a sister were true. The headmistress of the school that the oldest four children attended arranged for the two of us under five to appear at dinnertime to receive a free school dinner. These were stopped when the man sent to interview mam was refused entry to our house. He explained, on the doorstep, that all she had to do was to complete a form confirming he had made a visit, but he was sent away. The house was sparsely furnished and we only ever had two chairs so I asked why she had not let the man inside. I got the same response when I asked if it was true that a kind teacher, Miss Seabourn, who was leaving to be married wanted to adopt me and was refused. 'What would people have said?' Mam didn't want any authority to interfere with her life. She seemed afraid of consequences that she did not fully understand.

My escape from the misery at home was in books. I had learned to read early in childhood and my favourite place was the children's room at the library. My favourite smell for many years was the scent of furniture polish that was there in the clean, safe space where I would spend as much time as I could. I existed in the world inhabited by Tom

Sawyer and Huck, on the plantation with Uncle Remus's stories of Brer Rabbit and, a few years later in the simple funny days of W W Jacobs' *Port of London*. As a child I owned one book, a small flimsy copy of *Willow the Lame Deer*. It was my most treasured possession in a house where there were no books. My love of reading helped to separate me from my environment and also from my family. They thought I was very strange. My earliest memory was waiting and waiting for someone to come and take me home from a place where I never felt I belonged. My brothers and sisters thought that about me too, that I was not part of the family. I was told years later, 'We always thought mam had brought the wrong baby from the hospital.' In the books it seemed that children sat on mothers' laps while she read bedtime stories, brothers and sisters had fun and laughed. Not for us in real life though. Like many of the families around we never went away on holiday. Mam, who could hardly read or write, only ever once travelled on a train and once went to see a 'talkie' at the cinema. She fell asleep and didn't bother to go again. She didn't set foot in a bank because she never had any money.

We were clothed from a stall on the market that sold second hand stuff. It was a poor district and the cheapest coats and trousers were already well worn when they were passed on. Unlike the picture that most have of a home with many children my mam was no cook. The one dish we had time after time emerged from a stewpot, perpetually topped up, that stayed in the oven alongside the fire. On the odd occasion it received a tin of corned beef or the latest catch, such as a rabbit or hare, were thrown into its bulging shape but the common fill was potato. Lots and lots of potato and swede. Mam would sometimes make a pie. The pastry was always thick and solid in the form of a covering set to protect whatever the large dish held beneath. I would sit and suck the crust that gravy had failed to penetrate. I loved school dinners.

Then I encountered a real live miracle worker, Mrs Gunn. One day in Senior school, when I was twelve years old, we were given a blank sheet of paper and a pencil and told by the teacher to write about a boat on a lake. He must have had a warped sense of humour, we all lived a long way from the nearest lake. The picture that came into my mind must have been from my imagination. I could see a lake with a boat moving gently on a surface lit by the moon and covered with the reflection of a mesh of stars. I was sent for. Normally we were sent into the Headmaster's room by a teacher and caned, but on this occasion I was escorted there by his secretary, Mrs Gunn. Mr Harrison wore his familiar stern look as I was passed the writing I had done the day before. In front of the large desk I read, as commanded, my piece about the boat on the lake. I was interrogated about the writing. 'Where had I read this, how did I know, why a mesh of stars?' Then he nodded to her and I was led out into the corridor. 'Stay behind after school and come to see me here,' Mrs Gunn said. At half past four I still had no idea what was in store for me but I was ushered into an empty class-room and told to sit at a desk where a large book lay open. Mrs Gunn asked me to read to her. 'Oh, for a muse of fire,' it began and I was introduced to the Bard. Mrs Gunn must have seen the effect it had on me, this appeal to imagine: 'within this Wooden O' the armies and horses. 'Would you like to learn about this writing and about poetry and drama?'

And that was the beginning. She taught me how to project words and entered me into speaking competitions, took me to the theatre with her friends. This scruffy, raggedy little lad, with her beautifully dressed friends, was taken to see a play at the Theatre Royal in Nottingham. It was as if blinds had been drawn from high, wide windows and light flooded in to show me what life could hold. How could I ever settle to live in the darkness ever again?

Mrs Gunn produced a school play to compete in a local festival. It was 1951 and people were celebrating the Festival of Britain with all manner of entertainment. I played the part of Bottom in Shakespeare's play within the play *A Midsummer Night's Dream.* We won a large Cup and were commanded to perform at the Nottingham Albert Hall before a distinguished audience of local dignitaries. During rehearsals, and the performance to win first prize, I had worn a pair of PT shorts issued by the school. In the dressing room beneath the stage I quietly explained to Mrs Gunn that I had forgotten to bring my shorts. In my late forties, during one of my frequent visits to her home, she reminded me of the incident. 'I reassured you it would be all right to play the part with your underpants on, then realised by the look on your face you didn't have any. You were fourteen years old and had never worn any underwear. Do you remember what we did? I slid one of your legs down the sleeve

Gren Gaskell as Bottom (right) in the prize-winning school production of A Midsummer Night's Dream.

of your jumper then tied the rest around your waist.' I could remember clearly what she did and what she had said. In the final scene, when I went on stage to commit suicide after losing my beloved Thisbe, her instruction was ringing in my ears. 'Die very carefully, Pyramus.'

Mrs Gunn did not show the disappointment she must have felt when, eighteen years old, I left my factory job, married, and went to work in the pit. But she was there to help nine years later when I was desperate to leave. She recommended me to one of her friends for a temporary office job. I stepped into a different world.

When the conversation about my missing underpants took place I was sitting in her clean, warm, friendly home wearing one of my bespoke suits with clean white underwear beneath, laughing with the angel who had made such a difference to my life. And what a life! Now, very much thanks to her kindness, I think I am perhaps the luckiest and the happiest of men.

MRS GUNN

'A way with words.' That's what you said
So many, many years ago,
And as I stood in hand made suit
You saw the boy you used to know
In threadbare coat and scuffed up boots
The scruffy muffler at his throat
With all the others wearing shoes
That shone and ties and matching coat.
Was I alone so different then?
My words were different. When
You called my name
In your clear singing tone
I wondered first what I had done
To earn that walk to master's room
But the reassuring smile said soon
We shall discover who you are.
Yet I could never be the star
You had in mind. The Corn Was Green
But not for me and what you'd seen
Would take a lifetime to emerge
And when it came the words would surge
Forth in a spate and always run
To speak my grateful thanks to you
My Mrs Gunn

Gren Gaskell worked as coal miner for nine years until Mrs Gunn, his guardian angel, rescued him. Starting with a temporary office job with an insurance company he rose to become the head of an accounts office in Rugby. After being separated from his family for thirty-five years he was invited with Arline, his new wife, to attend his sister's funeral. One of Gren's brothers remarked to Arline that they always thought that their mam had brought the wrong baby home from the hospital. 'So it seems that I was as much a stranger to my family as they had been to me'.

EASTON WREN

Easton Wren was born in Prestwick, Ayrshire, in January 1938

It was July 1962. I was on an oil exploration camp in the Sahara of Libya near the ancient town of Ghadames. I loped along the desert runway, crunching through the mix of sand and gravel, wondering why I liked the Sahara so much, even in the noonday sun with the temperature commonly at fifty-four degrees Celsius (one hundred and thirty degrees Fahrenheit). The desert was clean and so quiet and as I ran, content with the easy gait and flowing endorphins, I wondered where my voyage of discovery would take me in the future.

This notion also caused me to think back in time, as far as I could remember, and with a sudden jolt I heard once again the shrill voice scream, 'Hurry! Hold my hand and come quickly!' Everywhere there was noise, panic and confusion in the darkness that engulfed me. 'Why does this always happen at night?' I wondered, but at three years of age I could be forgiven for not being remotely aware of the motive and mechanics of the Blitz in Glasgow in 1941.

I felt my hand in a vice-like grip and was pulled so fast down the dark, damp stairway that I was certain I would stumble and fall into the deep basement beneath the tenement building. We went deeper into the 'dunny', a word long transformed in the Scots vernacular from the original dungeon and which bore a striking resemblance to the original, albeit without the locks and chains and instruments of torture. It felt like a prison keeping people captive until it was safe to come out again.

Eventually the air raid sirens stopped and the quiet murmurings of the frightened women and children gradually rose in the anticipation of yet another reprieve. Then, like a flashing rapier, the beam of the air raid warden's torch cut through the darkness to herald the 'all clear' and the long awaited permission to return home. 'Why is it always at night?' I wondered again. If it happened in daylight you could see the aeroplanes and the bombs coming and it might be easier to run away from them, but in the dark you sat and waited like a frightened rabbit, hypnotized by the staring gaze of a predatory mamba.

At school the next day the teacher nervously counted the children by calling their names. One day, after a similarly frightening night-time episode, a pupil called Ellen was not in the classroom. I knew her well because we had been paired off by the teacher to hold hands going in and out of the classroom for breaks. The teacher explained how her nightie had caught fire the night before when she sat too close to an electric fire. I was not convinced and later found out that she had been killed with many others in the bombing.

I wondered what it would be like to be in a house hit by bombs, since I had seen so many bombed houses in our neighbourhood. The ruins and rubble offered many scrambling opportunities on our way to school.

The war brought many contrasts. There were few young men or even middle aged men about. Only one of my school chums had his father at home. He had failed to pass a medical for the army. All the other fathers, uncles and older brothers were 'away in the war'. Occasionally they would come home 'on leave' with stories about training and invasion and such. The radio played Glenn Miller music and gave reports on the fighting but I was never sure what it all meant. I dreamed often of planes and soldiers and ships and guns and what might happen if the Germans came. 'You will be a brave young soldier and kill them all,' the old ladies would tell me. I did not believe that I could do that but felt I might have to try. 'Why do they say that?' I wondered, 'Is it to protect me … or them?' The Blitz went on for almost a year.

In June of 1945 I was seven years old. I watched the adults having their parties in the streets to celebrate the end of the war. My father came home from the army with his kit, medals, stripes and souvenirs and a thousand stories to tell. I remember treating him as a stranger with questions like 'Who are you?' and 'Why do you want to live here?' This was in spite of the fact that my mother had kept his memory alive for several years with photos and read his letters to me. This must have broken his heart but, like all soldiers, after the terrifying experience of war the return to civilian life was peaceful but 'boring' and he found it hard to adapt. It took a long time for the family to get back to normal.

In 1946 in south-west Scotland on the Ayrshire coast, it was a record-breaking long, hot summer. The family spent the month of August at a small village called the Maidens where I met two brothers from another Ayrshire town called Darvel. One of them was a kindred soul called Bobby Taylor and we played together every day. (Later we were re-united at Glasgow University). We hunted for crabs and fished off the pier but the main attraction was the group of German Luftwaffe prisoners of war who lived in the camp along the beach from the village. They spent their summer days sitting on the sand, swimming, playing football and whittling pieces of wood into boats and animals. Eventually we spent most of the day with the prisoners who were waiting for repatriation and not considered to be of any risk. Bobby asked me how I would handle the Germans if they came at us with guns and the harsh reality of facing an armed enemy became obvious. Strange talk for eight-year-olds, but these were certainly strange times.

Where were the legions of healers who should have come out of the ashes and said to all the traumatized young ones, 'There, there, the war is over, you do not have to be afraid any longer, you are safe now.' The children were never considered in this light and this may have had

The Wren family (1941).

several consequences such as the 'Brain Drain' that took place when my generation was old enough and educated enough to say goodbye to Europe.

I continued to run in the Saharan sunshine, thinking about survival. If the temperature was like this in Scotland then, in one day, it would probably kill half the human and animal population. My thoughts wandered back to the effects of the war that I scarcely remembered. Presumably most young children at that time were frightened of dying at any moment, living with terror, seeing the fear in the eyes of the adults trying to protect us, and completely unaware of the reasons for it all and unable to cope. Perhaps we forget the trauma with time and, as functional adults, have learned to deal with the scars. We are now the last generation to have memories of these dreadful times and soon the story will sit in the history books and film clips as a series of factual events, but little, if any, of the children's experiences will be known.

Easton Wren in his Cub's uniform (1947).

The post-war years brought many changes and my parents often remarked about things they remembered from their childhoods and the prewar years such as bananas, Cornflakes, Kit Kat chocolates and so on. With time we were re-introduced to such delicacies, and even with the rationing of sugar, meat and chocolate that continued for some time, life eventually reached a stage by about 1952 where it seemed to be 'normal' and a far cry from my memories of the war. Houses which had been bombed and flattened were now removed and new developments took their place and the thrill of playing in the 'bombed houses' soon faded.

As youngsters in the post war years we were able to play games in the streets since there were few, if any, parked cars. This is one thing I noticed on later visits to Glasgow, after emigrating to Canada, where every side street was crammed with cars. I also remember the advent of television, the original small black and white, single channel edifice which few people were privileged to own. Education was important and there was little time for television since playing, school, and *The Goon Show* on radio offered more attractive pastimes.

Easton Wren graduated from Glasgow University with a BSc in Geology and a PhD in Geophysics. He worked in North and East Africa in oil and gas and mineral exploration before moving to Canada where he spent many years with large oil companies. Easton has his own consulting company and is also currently Exploration Vice President and Director of Americas Petrogas Inc.

Easton has taught courses in Canadian and American universities and is a former Distinguished Lecturer for the American Association of Petroleum Geologists.

'I appreciate very much today the quality of school and university education I received and the calibre of many of my elementary and high school teachers was exceptional. I cannot imagine it being in any way of a higher calibre today. I often wonder if I was part of the chosen generation to be educated and help to bring the country back to prosperity. However, I was also one of the young adults with a family who left the country with the expectation of greener pastures in Canada. Perhaps I needed to leave Europe for psychological reasons, namely the prospect of another war. Greener and safer pastures might have been the objective.'

ELISABETH DONNELLY

*Elisabeth Donnelly (née Edwards)
was born in Wallasey, Cheshire, in August 1939.*

When I arrived in the world Britain was about to go to war with Germany, so some of my earliest childhood memories are of the sound of air-raid warnings, an indoor Morrison Shelter on which I cracked my head open, and my father in his warden's uniform. Being in a 'reserved occupation' as an engineer's fitter with the local bus company my father was exempt from service in the Armed Forces; but he did his bit for the war effort on duty as an Air-Raid Warden, commanding folk to 'put that light out' and dowsing incendiary bomb fires with his trusty stirrup pump and bucket. My mother had a difficult time during my birth and was not in the greatest health during my early years, so my father packed us off to stay with my Aunty Chris and her baby son in Sudbrooke, a small village near Lincoln for large periods of the war. Thus it follows that some of the best memories of the forties for me, are not of Wallasey and the bombs and air-raids, but of an idyllic existence in the countryside of Lincolnshire where the only reminders of the dreadful events in the big cities were the Lancaster Bombers flying over on a sortie and an army barracks in the local park through which one could walk en route to the gravel pits for paddling. I vividly recall the rows of Nissan huts with their bright red fire buckets hanging outside. When the war was over, there were great celebrations and I remember standing at the top of Leasowe Road in Wallasey excitingly waiting for the 'Illuminated Bus' to pass by, with its rows and rows of light bulbs spelling out 'VE Day: Victory in Europe'. By then, being six years old, I was a pupil at St George's County Primary School so the visits to Sudbrooke had come to an end, but the

The Christening party.
A gathering of the Edwards clan to celebrate the christening of Elisabeth's brother David (1950).
Front row from left: Susan (Crane), Elisabeth, Nana Eddy, Richard.
Middle row: Geoffrey, James, Cecil, Janet (baby), Joan, John.
Back row: Thelma, Eric (Tulloch), Roland (Crane), Vera (Crane) Aileen (Tulloch), Nana Collcutt.

memories of that happy time have stayed with me forever.

In 1950 my parents presented me with a baby brother so no longer would I be 'an only child', a phrase that for some reason seemed to suggest to my childish brain that I was somehow different from my peers. What a surprise and a novelty he was to become to me and my curious friends as we pushed him around the neighbourhood in his high pram and helped mum at bath-time. I was ten at the time and to be given responsibility for a living, gurgling baby at such a tender age made me feel very important, though my brother often reminds me of the time I accidentally tipped him out of his pram when negotiating a particularly rocky path!

However, at ten I was still a child myself and the priorities of the day were 'going out to play' with the local children, usually in our quiet cul-de-sac but sometimes further afield and even close to a railway line; here we made dens in the track-side undergrowth and played games of Cowboys and Indians with bows and arrows made of twigs and string. I must confess to having been a total tom-boy which I blame on my boy cousins who were of a similar age and of whom I saw a lot in those bygone days. Their games were much more exciting than dressing dolls and pushing prams and, in any case, had I not joined in I would probably have been totally ignored.

Being reasonably good at spelling and fairly good at arithmetic I passed the eleven plus to one of the local grammar schools and my father, anxious to keep up with the trend of the time, rewarded my efforts with my first bicycle, a second-hand sturdy steed. I well remember the wooden blocks he made for the pedals so that I could reach, and his hanging on to the saddle as I wobbled nervously around the road endeavouring to stay upright. Eventually I had mastered the noble art of cycling and there was no holding me back. No destination was too far it seemed, until one day I found myself on the way to Chester. Only then did it dawn upon me that I had to cycle all the way back again, not that my parents would be worried. The fifties was a time of freedom for children without parents fearing for their safety. No, it was a question of whether I could make the distance back home! This little adventure did not however deter me from riding out to Bebington where two of my boy cousins, John and Richard, lived. They had a lovely big house where many family get-togethers took place and where we children indulged ourselves with games such as 'Sardines': when one hid and the rest searched and joined them in the hiding place, I seemed to be always the last one in! I'm afraid I was rather fearful of their father who I perceived as being terribly strict and not as loving as my own father, though at times he also ruled with a very firm hand. My aunt, however, was a wonderful hostess and her table always groaned with the most delicious goodies imaginable, something frequently recalled by senior members of the family in later years. When being entertained for dinner there were never fewer than four choices of vegetable to accompany the potatoes and roast and certainly at least three puddings to go alongside the apple pie with a choice of cream, custard or ice-cream.

It was two or three years into the 1950s when my parents allowed me to go away on holiday with my Aunt Joan and Uncle James and cousins, John, Richard and Janet to the most idyllic place I had ever seen. It was called Aberdaron, situated at the tip of the Lleyn Peninsula in North Wales. There were six of us and a large black Alsatian, called Ray. The journey itself was exciting and endless it seemed. Umpteen trains were boarded, and loaded and unloaded with our belongings until the end of

Feeding the chickens on the farm at Aberdaron. Elisabeth (centre) with cousins Richard and Janet (circa 1953).

the line at Pwllheli where we waited for a taxi to our final destination. We stayed on a working farm where arose wonderful opportunities to watch cows being milked, and to scatter food for the hens whose eggs we children were allowed to retrieve from under hedges and in the barn or from wherever these lovely free-roaming birds felt like leaving them. We were allowed to ride on the farmer's tractor at hay-making, though when I recall the necessary rabbit shoot and the subsequent gathering round the pit as they were skinned ready for the pot I really can't imagine I enjoyed such scenes and I certainly wouldn't now! As well as the farm adventures, there was the beach below to explore. This was accessed by steps roughly hewn into the cliff's side, probably made by farm boys in past generations, and as I recall was totally devoid of any other living soul. My childish mind served up episodes of Enid Blyton's 'Famous Five' although John, Richard and I only numbered three as toddler Janet was far too young to be allowed into our adventurous company and Ray was kept under close guard back at the farm. So just we three spent endless hours, skimming the smooth flat stones to see whose could make the most skips over the placid waters of the Irish Sea and often leaping the gentle waves with glee as they brushed the firm, soft sand. We could walk along the beach to Aberdaron and often did, though I don't remember there being much to see apart from watching the daily boat leave for Bardsey Island, a hump of land a few miles from the mainland. On one occasion, my aunt and uncle took us all on this quite sea-sick-invoking trip; it seemed this stretch of water our somewhat ancient boat had to negotiate, was the roughest in the entire Irish Sea! However, the trip was worthwhile as we were able to see close at hand, the hundreds of grey seals that inhabited the rocky waters surrounding Bardsey and the screaming gulls and other sea birds that nested on its cliffs. There wasn't much to see on the island: an old lighthouse, a derelict farm dwelling and some sheep.

One day, Richard and I, for John was quite involved in making himself useful around the farm, set off on an adventure of our own. My aunt had filled us with a plentiful breakfast and packed some sandwiches and a bottle of lemonade. Thus, armed with our picnic and little else, we set off for Whistling Sands near Nefyn, so called because when one walked across the soft dunes, the sand beneath one's feet would squeak and whistle which we thought was quite magical. I can't recall how far we walked that day or how we found our way there and back, we must have had a map of sorts but I relied upon my cousin with utter and complete faith in his abilities. I always hoped that he was equally impressed by my knowledge of the flowers and trees of the countryside, which I could name *ad nauseam.* Our pilgrimage to Whistling Sands took us all day, across unfamiliar terrain, but nobody seemed to have worried when we finally returned to the farm in the evening. That was how things were in the 1950s.

My knowledge and love of flowers was gained from my Lincolnshire Aunt Christine, with whom I stayed together with my Uncle Bill and cousin John Jago. I had spent many happy school holidays there and it was in Lincolnshire that I was able to indulge my passion for tree climbing and fishing for tadpoles and tiddlers in the local stream. My aunt taught us the names of every wild flower and in those days I was able to determine which wild mushrooms were safe to pick and eat and which to leave well alone. When not occupied up a tree or paddling in streams, John and I would sit on the roadside verge collecting car numbers, which passed infrequently in those days. On rainy days, we could be found in the kitchen making papier-mâché puppet heads, sitting by the Rayburn cooker for warmth. These would later be dressed by my aunt from old scraps of material in readiness for a puppet show to rival anything the 'Punch and Judy' man could produce at the seaside in New Brighton.

I was always an avid reader and I remember one birthday particularly because I was on holiday with my parents in a small Welsh village called Llansillin, staying in the local public house. Opposite the pub was a farm with a huge hay loft just by the gate. It was to this lofty perch that I retreated on a daily basis upon receipt of my parents' birthday gift, another book of adventure stories in which I could employ my more-than-vivid imagination and be oblivious to calls for tea. On the subject of reading, I remember my Lincolnshire cousin having a boys' comic publication called *The Eagle,* on the front of which were the colourful space-ship adventures of Dan Dare. How I envied him this comic, for the girls' equivalent of the time was entitled, unimaginatively, *Girl,* and somehow I never really took to it.

Another vivid memory of those halcyon days was the obligatory visit to my paternal grandmother who lived with her two unmarried sons, my uncles Austin and Cecil, in Egremont, a part of Wallasey bordering the River Mersey. Uncle Austin was vicar of a local parish church and their house was a rambling Victorian vicarage, the entrance to which was always, as far as I recall, via the back yard gate. On entering this gloomy abode one's nostrils were assailed by strange odours which at best could be described as unpleasant. I suspect it was left-overs from the kitchen area. The frontage of this rambling residence overlooked the River Mersey across a sloping garden on which was a rustic bench, though I don't remember actually sitting on it. We children were always confined indoors and occupied our time and relieved our boredom by observing passing ships, of which there were plenty on the river in those days, through brass binoculars strategically placed along the bay window-sills alongside framed photographs of other uncles in forces uniforms. The vicarage occupants later acquired a television set, the first members of the family to do so, a cumbersome affair which had to be viewed through a large magnifying glass placed in front of the screen.

One of the earliest family gatherings I can remember took place there as Nanna Eddy, as she was known to me, summoned us all, aunts, uncles and cousins, to watch the Coronation of Her Majesty Queen Elizabeth II in glorious black and white. I must say the arrival of a television set meant that the obligatory visit became somewhat more tolerable as I sat enthralled by Muffin the Mule and his friends on a Sunday afternoon before evensong at St Columba's.

As the fifities drew to a close I developed a passion for the cinema, of which there must have been six or more in Wallasey, thus providing plenty of choice to satisfy my interest. I had my favourite stars of course but was never allowed to have photos and posters up in my bedroom like today's youngsters. I suppose I was a dreamer, with my head in the clouds and a desire to become a famous actress, a notion soon squashed by my ever down-to-earth parents.

By the mid 1950s I was in my final year at grammar school and was permitted to go on a school trip to Holland, my goodness what an adventure and what fun that was. However, not being much blessed with academic prowess, my destiny was never going to be college or university so I was enrolled for twelve months in our Secretarial Sixth Form, to be taught the finer points of Commerce, Shorthand and Typewriting, Book-keeping, Geography and Spanish. The latter two subjects escaped much of my interest but I seemed to do well in the others, so with three O-levels, as they were called in those days, in English, Art and Domestic Science (cookery to you and me), plus my certificates in Typing and Shorthand, I stepped forward precariously into the big wide world of adulthood and earning a living.

On leaving Oldershaw Grammar School Elisabeth (Lis) Edwards obtained employment with Midland Bank. After a period of training she worked at branches in Birkenhead and Liverpool. She then became a tutor on Merseyside, training the bank clerks of the future. At this time she met her future husband, Douglas. Lis is an active member of her local church community, a passionate supporter of Liverpool FC and a lover of Cavalier King Charles spaniels.

'My deep love and knowledge of the countryside stem from those early childhood years in Lincolnshire.'

PATRICK FALLON
Patrick Fallon was born in Liverpool in March 1939

My paternal grandfather, Patrick Fallon, was a riveter in the Royal Navy dockyard at Queenstown in County Cork. He left Ireland in 1910, perhaps a hasty departure along the lines, 'You are to appear tomorrow in court, and the boat for Liverpool leaves tonight.' So at the age of five my father, also a Patrick, found himself transported to the banks of the Mersey. Today we might talk about a family of asylum seekers.

Within a few years young Pat was diagnosed as having tuberculosis, a virtual death sentence for the poor. The doctor advised plenty of meat and fresh air. On leaving the hospital his mother bought her son a pork pie: that was the end of the special diet. Honora had been a schoolmistress before she wed Pat's father. Nevertheless she decided to take her doomed nine-year-old out of school and keep him at home to turn the mangle. The Fallon mangle must have been out in the open, for Pat lived to eighty-four.

Kitty Ryan and Pat Fallon met in February 1936 and married in August. She was twenty-three and he was thirty-one. It was an arranged marriage: not at all forced, but definitely brokered. It's a good story, but no room for it here.

The Great Depression was well established by 1936. Unemployment and hopelessness were endemic, with few places in England worse off than Merseyside. Largely self-educated and by now a Customs Officer, Pat held the King's Commission. He had a promising and relatively well-paid job, and still lived with his parents and his six sisters and brothers. He was the only member of the family bringing any money into the house, so his decision to marry came as a shock to his many dependents.

His bride, the second of ten children, always moved like lightning, mentally and physically. She was a natural raconteur with a vivid turn of phrase, but for all practical purposes was probably dyslexic. Father would read aloud to her, as he later did to us, but she claimed never to have read a book to completion after leaving school.

Pat and Kay had eight children of whom I was the second born. The age gap between their first and last child is eighteen years. As father continued to rise in the Civil Service, so our childhood circumstances must have been strikingly different.

It took years for anyone to notice that my vision was very poor. Before my first pair of spectacles, at the age of six, I must have lived inside a sort of impressionist painting. The lenses, thick as the bottom of an old bottle, were an improvement on the hand that nature had dealt me, but the smudgy contents of the classroom blackboard remained a mystery. Nobody knew how little I saw and it was years before I was automatically put in the front desk. Even with glasses I remained fogbound and it never occurred to me or anyone else that further measures were needed. I managed to learn a surprising amount but, relevant or not, for the rest of my schooldays my place in class swung wildly between first and near last. If you are very short-sighted your brain probably has to work quite hard to make sense of whatever information turns up. You don't recognise faces until their owners get close, or open their mouths. Most sport is a dead loss. I rarely caught a ball, rarely hit one, and sometimes never saw it at all.

Our education was given a very high priority. We lived in a rented semi-detached four-bedroom house in Crosby, a Liverpool suburb. Up to the age of twelve we children were all sent to local fee-paying Catholic schools run by religious orders. All these schools required uniforms; our books and games kit had to be paid for.

After the first day or two I always walked to school alone, warned to take care crossing the roads and not to talk to strangers. Arriving late for school or with unpolished shoes or grubby sports kit were punishable crimes. Forgetting your homework, textbooks, dinner money or other necessities carried their own penalties. Getting us out of the house after breakfast – school satchel packed, fairly clean and nearly on time – was a whole industry in itself. And when I returned there were hours of written homework, corrections, and learning by heart, all to be done for next day.

John was my big brother, eighteen months older. He and I were a team. A fleeting familiarity with family dynamics will identify the captain. In our mid teens the balance started to change as our different strengths emerged in plainer sight: we were more like friends. John's commitment to study, his competitive spirit, and later his talent for finding parties were important influences. I am ashamed to recall that John and I probably did our best to exclude the younger ones from our joint projects. It came as quite a pleasant surprise to get to know them better as we and they started to grow up.

Most of our neighbours were kind and friendly. We must have provided them with some entertainment and interest, even if our use of the road as an adventure playground was noisy and disruptive. We children were offered gifts of outgrown toys and games from the 1930s, which were otherwise unavailable during the war. We also acquired cracked cricket bats, warped and gut-strung tennis rackets of peculiar profile, along with old copies of the Boys' Own Paper full of plucky stories set in distant jungles of the Empire or aboard tramp steamers imperilled by the machinations of dusky foreigners. These prizes were later supplemented by solar topees last worn under the Indian midday sun, the greenish dinner jackets of retired tea planters, and their creamy silk shirts.

On one occasion we were given a nineteenth century East India Company muzzle loading musket complete with its ramrod. We soon had this in working order, manufactured our own gunpowder, and (insanely) shot half inch steel ball-bearings a hundred yards along the alley behind our house.

Another noteworthy gift was a set of proper archery equipment. The yew bow was long and strong, the arrows with their feathered flights were tipped with bronze points. We collected from shops the bright red rectangular metal boxes in which packets of Oxo meat flavouring cubes were stored. John cut and shaped and punched the metal and fastened it together with the tiny nuts and bolts that were part of the Meccano toy construction sets that have now been superseded by Lego. His armourer's task complete, John kindly allowed me to be the first wearer of the gleaming flak jacket. Then came the part I had failed to foresee. I was also the testing ground for our new weaponry. I stood in the middle of our road, while John retired a suitably sportsmanlike distance, drew back and aimed the re-strung bow. The arrow thudded home and pierced my breastbone. The likely outcome was beginning to dawn upon me and I fled up the road, rattling and rattled. John had time to reload and loose off another lethal bolt, which this time failed to find flesh but dangled through my tin suit above the kidney. John may well have been subject to some parental correction for this fascinating experiment. I have no recollection of any retribution, except perhaps the fate due to a sneak and telltale.

Philomena appeared when I was three. She was bald for a long time, then specialised in running away. I was probably responsible for making sure she didn't. Paul followed on my fifth birthday. My response to the inevitable and fatuous remarks about my wonderful present was a curt 'Put him in the dustbin'. Despite this unpromising start our relationship improved.

In 1951 the exhausted post-war population had been treated by the Government to the Festival of Britain. A giant celebration was held to cheer us all up and impress the rest of the universe: its focus was design and manufacturing, architecture, entertainment and the arts. An exhibition site was established in central Liverpool on waste ground recently cleared by the Luftwaffe. I spent a day there with Paul. We were twelve and seven and queued up to go down simulated coal mines, admired the latest in aeroplanes and boats, and inspected extemporized production lines that turned out woolly white Dunlop tennis balls, packets of Tate and Lyle cane sugar lumps, or Boots cough mixture. We must have gazed at countless propaganda films. The highlight of this 'tonic for the nation' for Paul and me seems to have been a Lever Brothers' production line that manufactured and wrapped tiny tablets of toilet soap, the sort you find today in every hotel but a great novelty then. Paul and I toured the process repeatedly to collect our free samples at the exit. The staff soon saw through our disguises and clothing changes, laughingly gave us a parting bonus, and we returned home to mother with our pockets bulging.

We come now to the circumstances that transmuted the lives of the eight Fallon children. Our parents were totally committed to ensuring that we were properly educated and they considered that passing exams was our only route out of the Liverpool Irish ghetto. This approach had certainly worked for father. At the age of thirteen he was already on a red Post Office bicycle delivering telegrams; and during the Great War those small yellow envelopes invariably contained bad news. He went on to sit a succession of civil service examinations. In some, to use his own words, he was placed first in the Kingdom. When he retired from the public service father was Head of HM Customs in Liverpool.

My formal studies began in the kindergarden of Seafield Convent in Crosby. Despite mother's own educational struggle she did not spare me from pre-school tuition. Seated on her knee in front of the morning room fireplace, together we sounded out the headlines from the Liverpool Echo. Thus I learned to read at four and a half years old, before I put on my first school uniform.

In 1945 I transferred to the preparatory school for St Mary's College in Crosby run by the Irish Christian Brothers. Thus began a generally enjoyable twelve years of education. Its most striking feature, literally, was the generosity with which the leather strap was used to foster our studies. This teaching aid was about a foot long, an inch wide, and one third of an inch thick; stitched, fairly flexible with a shaped grip. Every teacher had one, but some preferred to employ whatever weapon came to hand. Others did not use it at all or only sparingly: their restraint was overshadowed by the enthusiasm of the floggers. As a group our Irish Christian Brothers seemed more violent than the lay masters. They probably had much to put up with, living in community with the other Brothers and their vows of celibacy. A number bordered on savagery but others were the gentlest of men.

My parents did not take exception to our many, sometimes daily, beatings. Indeed, I remember hearing mother say to one teacher, 'If he gives any trouble, Brother, strap him.' I was being brought up in a seemingly barbarous world, but violence was an accepted part of our culture. We knew that beatings were more common in our school than in others, but in a curious way it seemed normal and I doubt that my teachers were sadists.

Ironically, I was later to become responsible for the development of the Ministry of Education's policies on behaviour problems in English schools. Truancy, of which I had no knowledge, was one. So too was corporal punishment, of which I probably had more experience than any civil servant in Whitehall.

Some among the Brothers might have been unhinged in various ways, but I never experienced any sexual abuse or heard of any inflicted on my fellow pupils. These men had chosen the religious life and had joined an order founded to provide education for the barefooted boys who roamed the streets of Cork in the nineteenth century. The Brothers who were sent to teach in England might have been the pick of the bunch. They were all graduates, often from modest backgrounds themselves. They cared about us.

The Irish Christian Brothers made no attempt to promote Irish history or to resist English jingoism, apart from our Roman Catholic version of the Reformation. Whatever the grim history of Ireland, the Brothers went in for no nationalism whatever.

To enter the main school at St Mary's College I had to pass the eleven plus examination. The four entry forms absorbed about one hundred and fifty twelve-year-olds. We came from the nearby farms, suburbs and slums, a great mix of cultures, classes, and different accents, deprivation and domestic comfort. Our language at school was based on two distinct dialects. The unmistakeable urban sound of Merseyside known as Scouse; instead of you and yours the boys from the Dock Road used words like 'youse', 'yiz' and 'yer'. Typically their migrant surnames were McCann, McGlone, Shaughnessy or O'Malley; a few Welsh incomers called Jones or Hughes; and the odd Uruburu. The other dialect was an archaic burr from the surrounding flat farmlands, rich with 'thee' and 'thou' and odd usages such as 'Borrow uz tha' pen'. Was this the immemorial sound of isolated Lancashire Catholic families untouched by the Reformation? Its speakers bore the surnames of their towns and hamlets: Formby, Ford, Holt, Lunt, Preston. After a couple of years in the same classroom we all sounded alike, upmarket scousers.

The school met in full assembly every morning at nine, to sing hymns and recite prayers, listen to notices, and hear the glories of the school teams; sometimes to witness punishment. Every forty minute lesson started and ended with a prayer, and each classroom was surveyed by a crucifix and a large painted plaster statue of Our Lady. The final lesson of the morning was Religion and lasted thirty minutes only. Taken by our Form Master it was usually but not invariably devoted to spiritual matters.

The Brothers dressed in long black cassocks belted with wide cloth sashes and wore tall stiff circular Roman collars. Most of the lay teachers were men. Some wore suits and some wore jackets with sober trousers. All wore ties. Floating black academic gowns were optional. Pupils were addressed by surname only, and we spoke to each other likewise. I sat at the same desk in the same classroom all year and for every lesson, except for classes in the gymnasium, the Music, Art and Woodwork rooms, gardening, the library or laboratories. Our teachers did the moving.

Our curriculum was broad, with many extra opportunities to make things, play games, pursue hobbies, learn languages, attend film shows and lectures, visit factories, read newspapers, act in plays, help in the book-room, take part in debates. Some extras were less optional than others: choir, orchestra, team practices, and moving school furniture.

Many of our lay teachers had fought in the war, typically as navigators in Lancaster and Wellington bombers high in the lethal frozen night skies over occupied Europe. Having survived this near fatal apprenticeship, they were tough, quick and entertaining, addicted to cigarettes, decorated but unwilling to talk about their experiences. With some shame I can recall an attempt to divert Mr Hanlon from teaching us Chemistry. The worst job in a bomber was rear gunner and I asked Joe if he had ever lost one on a mission. The snarled answer exploded like an eighty-eight milimetre shell: 'We took him out in cobs,' he rasped.

Our education at St Mary's was divided like Gaul into three parts: examinations, religious doctrine, sport. Ball games and thick spectacle lenses do not go together. But I tried. I bought my own willow cricket bat and hard red leather ball, but cannot recall scoring a single run, taking a single catch, or bowling a single wicket. The school employed a professional tennis coach: no point for me. Rugby was better. I was big and useful at pushing in the second row of the scrum. I quite enjoyed this and bought my own jock strap and yellow leather scrum cap. Eventually I played for the second fifteen. I don't think I ever caught the ball in a lineout, even on a dry day, but from time to time I injured a member of the opposing team, and very occasionally heaved myself and the ball across the line to score a try. I was taught to swim by Mr Simpson, a former Royal Navy officer who also ran the Crosby Sea Scouts. The venue was the Balliol Road swimming baths in Bootle, where my watch was quickly stolen from the changing rooms while I was wallowing in the water at the end of a rope secured by Mr Simpson, who had only one arm. Without my glasses I could not see him or his gestures. I could not recognize anyone or any thing in the pool. It was no good.

At fourteen I drifted into athletics and became good at throwing things. You do not need to see clearly to throw the discus, put the shot or hurl the hammer. I was soon chosen for school teams. In my years as an under eighteens athlete I regularly brought home medals from the Lancashire County Championships. One wondrous summer Saturday in June 1957 at White City Stadium in Manchester I won the Northern Counties AAA hammer event and the discus and set new records in both which lasted a surprisingly long time. I was fourth that year in the national hammer rankings and the Amateur Athletic Association placed me under the supervision of Denis Watts, the national Olympic coach.

Patrick Fallon prepares to fire a twelve pound cannon ball sixty yards. *Manchester Evening News*, 1957.

The transition at eighteen to adult athletics failed to maintain these triumphs. Indeed it nearly ended my university career. In my first year at Liverpool University I was the only member of the athletics team to win an event in the Christie Cup, our annual key fixture against Leeds and Manchester. This was soon followed by well deserved appearances before the University Senate Committee on the Satisfactory Progress of Students. They reluctantly allowed me to re-sit the examinations I had failed. Effectively this was the end of my sporting career. Getting on with your studies took first place.

Throughout my childhood the family was short of money. In the school Easter holidays, just turned fourteen, my first paid job was to help the milkman. Nobody owned a refrigerator and fresh milk did not keep well in the warm months. Every morning we made horse-drawn deliveries of chilly pint and half pint bottles of milk onto the sleeping doorsteps of Crosby. Mr Parrington asked what wage I wanted. Schooled no doubt by mother in the cut and thrust of the job market: 'Ten shillings a week,' I bid. The dairyman in his long brown overall coat took me on with no evident qualm. I had to rise at four o'cock. Mrs Parrington gave me bread and jam in the dairy when we came back about nine o'clock to reload the float to continue the round. By noon we had washed the clanking empty bottles and refilled them with the morning milk for next day's delivery. I asked for and got a fourfold rise to two pound a week when I came back to work in the summer break.

Mr Parrington would give me the reins to drive our two-wheeled cart along the last hundred yards of Jubilee Road. I could whip Billy up to a spanking trot and whoa him to a stop before turning him round where the road met the railway. This bottle shaking treat was actually quite dangerous. Jubilee Road was a long straight ravine of joined up houses. The front doors and their scoured steps gave straight onto narrow pavements which swarmed with children.

The milk bottles were embossed with the name of our dairy in red or green. The top was a waxed two inch cardboard circle pressed into the recess in the neck. This snug disc had a perforated centre, which you could poke down and fish the top off with your finger through the hole: quite a pleasing manoeuvre. Empty milk bottles were not always properly rinsed out, a neglect that still offends me half a century later.

You always ended up with some empties that belonged to competing dairies. Every few weeks I had to return these mavericks and round up our own. The errant empties went into a low metal basket over the front wheel of the delivery bicycle. I dropped them off at their proper homes around Crosby then wobbled back with our own straying bottles.

Another of the milk lad's duties was to take the horse to have its shoes replaced at the forge in the centre of Crosby. I walked Billy on the lead rein about half a mile along what was a busy main road in the 1950s. The smithy was soot black within, its fire goaded by bellows into an orange inferno. Horses were tethered near the anvil and sometimes jumpy. The blacksmith in his leather apron lifted each hoof in turn into his lap, prised off the old shoe, trimmed the excess growth off the hoof with a sharp knife, then filed it down with a great metal rasp. Each shoe was made to size before the wearer's eyes. The smith chose a flat bar of iron, heated it bright red and hammered it into a curve around the glittering anvil, heated it red again and punched nail holes through the bar, offered it up to its new user in a cloud of smoke like burning chicken feathers, finished off the shaping, and plunged the shoe into a water bath to cool it down. The scary final part comes when the blacksmith whacks six nails right into the horse's hoof with his hammer to fix the shoe in place.

Subsequent holiday work was likewise educational. My summer job in 1954 was on the local bright yellow vans – sometimes electric – of the Pioneer Laundry. The following year I helped to deliver bread around the barren and uninspired housing estates of Merseyside. Many of the regular van drivers were army trained and keen to pass on what they had learned in life and in uniform. This included illegal driving lessons. So, not licensed and no doubt uninsured, I jerked and stalled the bread van and its remaining cream buns along our customers' baking concrete streets.

In 1955 I started a series of short term Christmas jobs with the Post Office, helping to cope with its annual avalanche of Christmas cards, first as a sorting clerk and later as a temporary postman. The Crosby Postmaster appointed me his personal assistant so I was mostly spared delivery duties: no carrying a heavy mailbag around a freezing wet 'walk' populated by ill-numbered houses and hostile dogs. It was an early start, but once snug indoors, I did odd jobs around the sorting office, clocked the other 'temps' on and off duty, issued their numbered armbands and distributed Registered Letters. I drank lots of tea and enjoyed long conversations with the highly committed and erudite regular postmen. One year I picked up an extra week's work after Christmas and was sent to shift mountains of delayed mailbags and parcels down on the docks, a fascinating subculture where I think we did more work than the Liverpool dockers, witty and notorious skivers.

The family was at various times markedly short of money. But in the English class system one's values are more significant than hard cash. My problem was that I simply did not feel quite English enough. When I was a teenager, English by birth but Irish by blood, my integration seemed incomplete. I did not feel I was really accepted in that part of society to which I probably belonged by virtue of my education and father's professional status. Perhaps this feeling of not fitting in was my own version of adolescent identity anxiety: 'Who am I?' and 'Why am I me?'

The Irish had come in force to mainland Britain in the nineteenth century, often brutally displaced during the Potato Famine, ill-educated and impoverished, and the wrong religion for good measure. Today the ethnic Irish are generally assimilated, and demographers pronounce that they are indistinguishable in educational and socio-economic terms from the population as a whole.

As a child our relative poverty was brought home to me in the grocer's shop. It was common to be sent off to 'get the messages' from eight or nine years old. We made our main purchases at a shop called Duckell's and settled the total on a monthly account. We had problems in doing so from time to time and I was briefed one day by mother on how to deal with the feared reminder from the manager that we had fallen into arrears. I cannot recall that Mr Hopwood actually suggested that my mother might come in herself rather than send an innocent child with the shopping list. But I seized some opportunity to deliver my lines and piped up 'Put it on the account, Mr Hopwood, we are not leaving the district.' The astonished Mr Hopwood asked me to repeat this instruction, and waved me away from his counter as he struggled to conceal his mirth.

Patrick Fallon graduated from Liverpool University with a modest degree in Chemistry, but six years later was awarded a Doctorat de l'Université in Crystallography from the Sorbonne, rated 'très bien'. In 1967 he took what he intended to be a temporary position in the Civil Service and stayed thirty-three years in diverse policy posts at home and abroad, in the fields of science, education and cultural affairs. Patrick is married to Sally, whom he met in Paris, and they have four children.

This is an edited extract from a memoir on the individual childhoods of the Fallon brothers and sisters over some four decades of the twentieth century, for publication in August 2012. The provisional title is *Crosby … Fitting In*. Copyright © P J Fallon 2012.

ROBIN ELLIS
Robin Ellis was born in Sennen, West Cornwall, in June 1943

I come from Cornish tin mining stock with most of my uncles having been miners. My father, Joe, was an exception. He had been declared unfit for military service and worked as builder's labourer during the war. My mother was a full-time housewife, but carried out local part-time work when family responsibilities permitted. I had two elder brothers, Joe and Eric and a younger sister, Sally. An extended family of uncles, aunts and cousins lived nearby. Our house had a reasonably sized back garden in which we kept chickens and a ferret, in addition to growing vegetables of all sorts.

I went to Sennen Infants School while my brother Eric was in the juniors in an adjacent classroom. I wanted to go with him, I grabbed hold of the handles of two doors and had to be prised away. My infant teacher was 'Ma' Rowe who, like most teachers of the day, was a stern disciplinarian. The cane was often used. In winter we had milk delivered in bulk and it was warmed in a bath-pan on top of the coal-burning fire in the classroom. I had ginger hair and was, of course, teased mercilessly. As was the school fatty and the only black boy in the village. In the playground we played 'kingy'. This game involved the boy who was 'it' trying to hit the other boys with a ball. You could avoid being hit, and captured, by fending off the ball with your fist. We also played rounders and tended the school garden.

Both my brothers and later my sister passed the eleven plus examination and went to grammar schools in Penzance. I didn't and attended Cape Cornwall Secondary Modern, travelling to school in ancient buses. In winter we prayed for snow and ice which would give us days off.

Summer holidays were the best part of my childhood. I learned to swim at the sea end of the lifeboat slipway at Sennen Cove and Billy George and I built camps in what had probably been World War Two slit trenches at Rabbits Rock overlooking the sea. I would also help Uncle Willy at nearby Tower Farm. At one time he worked a pair of white Shire horses and later owned a Fordson tractor. Harvest and threshing were the best times to help on the farm as food was provided.

Food rationing was in place for the first ten years of my life. 'Boughten' food would have included bread and general provisions, Occasionally a pasty was purchased from Tommy the roundsman and even rarer still would be a fish and chip meal in a café in Penzance on one of our bus trips there. Generally, we ate beef during the year and only ate chicken at Christmas. Later it became the opposite. Rabbit pie was a real treat and it was 'off-ration' which was a bonus. Household water came from three sources. Drinking water was obtained from the chute in Sunny Corner, or from a well or pump from two other sites in the village. Rainwater collected in butts was used for laundry and other purposes.

The toilet arrangements were, by today's standard, bog standard. It was a WC (without water) of the 'bucket and chuck it' system. Even then we were recycling newspaper! I fancied myself as a singer, I was in the church choir for goodness' sake! Whilst using the outside amenity I would practice my singing. The WC was back-to-back to number three Sea View's WC and number three was the home of Granny Braunton and her grandson Leonard. Granny was always complaining about some illness or other and took to her bed often, expecting imminent departure. So one fine day yours truly was upon the 'throne' singing loudly when my mother overheard Granny B shout out, 'Leonard, Leonard, come quickly I'm dying. I can hear the angels singing.' I never did find out how she knew what angelic singing sounded like. The contents of the WC were deposited in a deep hole at the bottom of the garden, When full my father would split rhubarb crowns and plant them on top! The growth of this rhubarb was extremely vigorous, as you can imagine. After forty years of marriage I still have difficulty in convincing my wife 'I don't like rhubarb!!'

Father would go hunting in the autumn and winter on local farmland, with permission of course. His friend Nicky Tregear would often accompany him, as did I. We used the ferret and net system. Our ferret, Andy, would be put into the rabbit warren with a bell round his neck and in theory chase the rabbits into the net over the holes. Occasionally Andy would catch a rabbit and settle down in the burrow and eat it. My father and his mates described this as 'the ferrets gone to lie in'. Dad used to have to sit around trying to entice Andy out and occasionally resorted to digging him out. You could say that dad was not a happy bunny when this happened. Dad used to dispatch the netted rabbits with an efficient chop to the neck.

One Saturday when I was about eight years old I was carrying the net box and ferret box when I fell into a bramble patch and couldn't get up. Dad and Nicky thought it was ever so funny. Dad told me to get out of it, which I did by using the boxes as guards to protect my hands. No risk assessment then!

Out of County, even out of parish, was exploring. Mother, Sally and I went to Plymouth around 1950 to visit relatives. I can remember seeing what I later found out were bomb-damaged buildings. The only other 'out of county' trip, about three years later, was with mother to RAF Locking near Weston-super-Mare when my brother, Eric, was 'passing out' of the Apprentice Wing.

Robin Ellis left school at the age of fifteen and attended the National Training School in Gravesend before joining the Merchant Navy. His first voyage was on a vintage tanker to the Caribbean and the USA. He rose from a catering boy to able bodied sailor. After four years at sea he joined the Cornwall Constabulary and was posted to different parts of the county, eventually becoming a sergeant in Camborne. At one time he acted as an observer for the police helicopter in Cornwall. 'Not bad for a failed eleven-plusser to have served on Land, Sea and Air.'

Robin is married to Anne-Marie and they have a daughter, Louise, and a son, Laurie Joe.

BARRY WILLS
Barry Wills was born in Ashton-under-Lyne, Lancashire, in November 1945.

My early years were remarkably unremarkable, and in no obvious way prepared me for a life in the international minerals industry, which would take me to over forty countries, meeting people of different colours and cultures. Britain during my formative years was only beginning to experience the mass waves of immigration, and I have no recollection of speaking to a non-white person until I landed in Africa in late 1969.

I was born in the Lancashire cotton-mill town of Ashton-under-Lyne, six miles from the centre of Manchester. My father, Edward (Ted) Wills, was a Londoner, from Peckham, who had been transferred to the army barracks at Ashton in 1943, during the Second World War. It was here that he met, and married my mother, Marjorie Butterworth, and they settled in Ashton after the war.

We were a typical working class family, the first four years of my life being spent with my parents, and maternal grandparents in their general store, bought with my grandfather's family inheritance. Although running a small back-street shop was no easy life, it must have seemed Utopia to my grandparents who had experienced some privation in their married life.

In his youth grandad had joined the newly formed Territorial Army, the volunteer reserve force of the British Army, and on the outbreak of the war, he was sent to France with the Ninth Battalion of the Manchester Regiment, as part of the British Expeditionary Force. In 1915 he was in Turkey, fighting in Gallipoli. Whilst taking part in a raid on a Turkish trench he found that, on reaching their objective, all his comrades had been either killed or wounded. Retreating to his home trench he was shot in the back, and lay with the dead. As the bodies were eventually removed he stirred in the hot sun and someone noticed that he was still alive. Remarkably, less than a year later, he was back in the trenches, in the Battle of the Somme.

The legacy of war was that he was left with only one lung, but his troubles were exacerbated when, shortly after returning home, he lost his gas-fitting job after joining a strike at his works. For over ten years he was 'on the dole' receiving unemployment benefits, introduced just after the war. At that time this involved 'doling out' charity in the form of food, blankets, supplies and funds. This must have been a particularly hard period, as he and gran had three young children to raise. At one time, he and a friend walked all the way to Blackpool and back (roughly one hundred and twenty miles), in an abortive attempt to find work. They tried to make ends meet, with gran supplementing their meagre means-tested income by taking in washing and by house

Barry and friends outside the shop, November 1949.

cleaning for the relatively better off local people. Around 1930, grandad at last found employment, when a relative offered him a labouring job, dyeing leather in his factory. This was arduous work, involving standing over a large vat dipping the leathers, but kept him employed until he and gran took over the shop in 1949.

Short and stocky, grandad, despite his disability, had to have been a tough character to have lived the life he did. This is borne out by stories of him carrying out self-surgery on a large cyst on his neck, using an open razor, and catching a rat with his bare hands in the washing boiler shed!

Cobbled streets, back-yards, outside lavatories: these are some of my most vivid memories of life in the early fifties. Although mum and dad lived at the shop for only a few months, I spent many hours there, as school was only a couple of minutes walk away, and for the first few years of my schooling, lunchtime was spent at the shop. I particularly remember the wind-up gramophone and its box of needles, and scratchy arias from *La Bohème,* sung by gran's favourite tenor, Gigli.

Grandma was the family matriarch. Her wonderful Lancashire recipes are now vague memories: gelatinous cow heel pie, suet puddings cooked in muslin rags, pea soup and dumplings, but she was also the family medicine woman. The National Health Service was founded only in 1948, which eliminated the cost of treating illnesses, but it was still a tradition that common illnesses, particularly those suffered by children, were treated at home. The dreaded diseases were the life-threatening ailments such as scarlet fever, diphtheria, meningitis, polio and tuberculosis but for the 'ordinary' diseases, including measles, chicken pox, mumps and whooping cough, a doctor was called only if the situation became serious. In fact, families were so resigned to the inevitability of these diseases, that children were often deliberately exposed to active cases in order to 'get it over with'.

Grandma's medical chest contained an array of noxious brews, evil-smelling medicines and tonics, their perceived efficacy being directly related to the degree of foulness of taste. I was regularly given a dose of cod liver oil and malt, and on Friday nights the dreaded 'working medicine' a dose of a strong laxative of syrup of figs. Keeping the bowels 'moving' was all important, no matter that no problems in that area had been reported. Needless to say, Saturday morning were spent in fairly close proximity to the house!

Hospitals were to be feared. Often housed in nineteenth century work-houses, typical of those famously exposed by Charles Dickens in *Oliver Twist,* these places had the smell of death and decay. Even now I find the sight of large, dark, dimly lit buildings disturbing, probably sub-consciously recalling my time in hospital in the early 1950s, in a ward with several other children enduring tonsillectomies. As far as I know, I had never had tonsillitis, but it was common practice for children to have tonsils removed at an early age, probably because of the prevalence of throat infections.

Maybe even more feared was the dentist. Tooth extractions were bearable, being performed under general anaesthetic, but no such relief was available for the dreaded fillings, performed with a very slow, pulley-operated drill. No wonder that many young women in their mid-teens opted to have all their teeth removed and replaced by a false set. I remember my grandma informing her younger sister that it was time that her daughter had her teeth out.

A regular visitor to our cobbled back streets was the rag-and-bone man, with his horse and cart rattling over the cobbles, and his familiar call of 'rag-bone', simplified by time to an unintelligible, but unmistakable 'raa-boh'. He would collect old rags, for converting into fabric and paper, bones for making glue, scrap iron, old jam jars and other items in return for items of limited value. We children would often trade such items for goldfish and balloons, but the women of the district would eagerly await his supply of much-needed 'donkey-stones'.

Donkey-stones were soft scouring stones, originally used in the textile mills to provide a non-slip surface on greasy staircases. The stone took its name from one of the earliest manufacturers, Reads of Manchester, who produced a stone with a trade name of 'Read's Donkey Brand', so named because of the hard work performed by the stone, which was made from pulverised sandstone, cement, bleach powder and water. Working class women had hard lives of drudgery and routine, and the donkey-stoning ritual, which was unique to northern England, was an essential part of their weekly routine. Tuesday might be window-cleaning, while Wednesday might be devoted to cleaning the rarely used front parlour, but one day would be devoted to going down on hands and knees and donkey-stoning doorsteps, windowsills, the flagged kitchen floor, and most importantly, the paving stones, or 'flags', outside their terraced homes. 'Sanding the flag' was an ideal occasion for neighbourly gossip, but women were proud of their donkey-stoning, and would feel that anyone whose step was not meticulously sanded would have let the street down. One by one the donkey-stone factories closed down, the last being in Ashton-under-Lyne in 1979.

Monday was the traditional washing day, with drying in the winter months often taking the whole week. Washing was an arduous task, using a dolly-tub and mangle. Only cold water was piped to the house, which had to be ladled by hand into a copper tub and then heated for the day's wash. Clothes then had to be stirred about in the water, using a wooden stirrer, or 'dolly', to remove the dirt, and some items, such as white collars on Sunday shirts, needed prior scrubbing on a wash-board. Whites, especially white cottons, were boiled, and got a tiny dose of 'dolly blue' dye to enhance their brilliance. The washed clothes then had to be mangled to get the water out. This was a hot, steamy job calling for strength to lift the wet, heavy material out of the tub, using sprung wooden tongs, and skill to feed enough of the cloth into the rollers for the mangle to get a grip. More effort was then needed to turn the handle and squeeze the clothes through the rollers. Finally, the washtub had to be emptied by hand. If the weather was too bad to get the clothes out onto the washing line, they hung round the house on clothes horses or on 'pulleys' hung from the ceiling over the kitchen stove, getting in everyone's way. Once clothes were almost dry the creases had to be removed, so they were pressed with a series of flat-irons heated on the stove or by the fire and finally left in the open to dry naturally, or 'aired' before being put away until needed.

Coal was king in Britain and directly or indirectly fuelled our terraced homes. In winter the large fireplace provided heat for the room and a means of boiling pans of water placed on the open grate. The coal we used was cheap, low grade and dirty, producing much ash and soot, the airborne particles contaminating buildings and people alike. The Victorian buildings of the industrial north had black facades, highlighting their gothic gloominess, and it was only in later years, well after The Clean Air Act, 1956 that their original sandstone surfaces were restored in all their glory.

Many homes, including ours, also had stoves and washing tubs fuelled by coal gas (town gas). Ashton, like many industrial towns, had its own gas-works, where coal from the numerous collieries was heated to drive off the gas. The gas was collected in large reservoirs, or gasometers, from where it was piped to local industry and houses, and the residue was coke, a clean but expensive fuel.

The burning of coal in homes and industry produced another hazardous side-effect. Lancashire is noted for its rainfall, and the subsequent high humidity provided ideal conditions for minimisation of the breakage of threads in the cotton mills. However humidity and cold winters often produce fog, which combined with the coal-contaminated atmosphere, produced that dreaded combination of smoke and fog known as smog. This was a noxious mix of particulate matter and gases such as sulphur dioxide and nitrogen dioxide. Often a sickly yellow-green colour, these 'pea-soupers' would sometimes totally shut down the activities of a town, but I remember vividly walking to and from school when the visibility was an acceptable metre, with car headlights appearing slowly and eerily out of the gloom. Only towards the end of the fifties did the situation improve, with Clean Air Acts identifying 'smokeless' zones, where only smokeless fuels such as anthracite and coke could be burned.

For two weeks of every year drudgery and grime could be forgotten in the annual family holiday. Holidays in Blackpool with gran and grandad were the highlights of the early fifties. We always stayed in the same accommodation, or 'digs', near the tram sheds. Blackpool was in its heyday, unashamedly vulgar and brash, attracting the factory workers of northern Britain, particularly Lancashire's mill workers. With its famous tower, inspired by the Eiffel Tower, and fun fair, and trams shuttling up and down the long promenade, it was a magical place. However, Blackpool suffered some deprivation in the 1960s with the arrival of cheap air travel, and the subsequent popularity of the Mediterranean coast. Nevertheless, I still have fond nostalgic memories of the town, particularly of its three piers, where variety shows would

ONE HUNDRED YEARS OF CHILDHOOD

On holiday in Blackpool, with grandparents, dad, sister (Pat) and mum (1952).

Whit walks, Ashton (1955).

attract the most popular entertainers of the day, such as Morecambe and Wise, Tommy Cooper and Max Bygraves.

Regular Sunday school supplemented my five days at Holy Trinity School. Sunday schools are not recognised educational establishments, they merely attempt to offer religious instruction, and were originally designed to prevent children in the slums descending into crime. Once a year my Sunday school would participate in a uniquely northern custom, the annual Whit Walk, or 'Scholars' Walk'. The period around Whit Sunday, the seventh Sunday after Easter, is known as Whitsuntide. A procession from each church or Sunday school, accompanied by a band, would make its way to the centre of Ashton, with the children carrying baskets of flowers, or ribbons attached to banners, where a combined service would be held, with hymns accompanied by one of the brass bands. The church groups would then process along a route around the packed town centre before walking back to their own starting points. One of the traditions of the Whit Walks was for those taking part to wear new clothes for the occasion, and relatives would give us money 'for our new clothes'. Also people watching the walk would look out for people they knew to run forward and give them money.

In 1950, a year after the birth of my sister, Pat, we left the shop and moved to a new council estate, where mum and dad would live for the rest of their lives. Council houses were built and operated by local councils to supply well built homes on secure tenancies at below market rents to primarily working class people. Living in the new house must have been heaven, with no less than two indoor toilets and front and back gardens.

The life of a child in those days was simple. There were no home computers, and few people had televisions; we were the first in our street to own a television, bought to watch the Queen's Coronation in 1953, and people crowded into our house to view the flickering images on the twelve inch screen. 'Playing out' was the thing. Like most youngsters I was passionate about sport, and we played football in the street in winter, and then swapped the heavy leather ball for the cricket bat and ball in the summer. I was an ardent Manchester City supporter and to play football for your favourite team was every boy's dream. In the fifties players would stay with one team for life, and most of the Manchester City team were local boys made good, but not all of them. My boyhood hero was Bert Trautmann, the German goalkeeper, who like my dad had moved to Lancashire during the war, but for entirely different reasons.

Trautmann joined the Luftwaffe early in the Second World War, serving as a paratrooper. He fought at the Eastern Front for three years, earning five medals including an Iron Cross. Later in the war he was sent to the Western Front, where he was captured by the British as the war drew to a close. He was transferred to a prisoner-of-war camp in Lancashire and after the war refused an offer of repatriation. Instead he settled in Lancashire, combining farm work with playing as goalkeeper for the local football team, St Helens Town. When his side played Manchester City in a friendly in 1949, Trautmann was so impressive that the First Division side immediately signed him and wasted no time in putting him into their first team. The club's decision to sign a former Axis paratrooper sparked protests, with twenty thousand people attending a demonstration. Over time he gained acceptance through his performances in the City goal, playing all but five of the club's next two hundred and fifty matches.

Trautmann entered football folklore in 1956 with his performance in the FA (Football Association) Cup Final against Birmingham City. It was not for any outstanding save on a day when City were generally in control but for yet another example of his remarkable bravery and courage. With fifteen minutes of the match remaining Trautmann suffered a serious injury after diving at the feet of Birmingham City's Peter Murphy. Despite his injury he continued to play, making crucial saves to preserve his team's three to one lead. His neck was noticeably crooked as he collected his winners' medal; three days later an x-ray revealed it to be broken. Bert Trautmann was a heroic figure in every sense, and an inspiration to me, in that no matter what a person's background or circumstances, respect can be earned with self-belief and determination.

Our life was one of routines, and a calendar wasn't necessary to know the day of the week, as the evening meal was always the same on any particular day; I remember Mondays being beef pudding without fail! The evening meal in working class Lancashire was 'tea', lunch being the mid-morning snack, and the midday meal was dinner. Later, as I progressed up the social ladder, it was strange at first for dinner to suddenly become lunch, and tea dinner. Now well accustomed to the changes, I still cannot come to terms at all with an invitation for supper, rather than dinner. Supper in my mind has always meant a cup of warm milk and a biscuit before bedtime.

One 'teatime' stands out vividly in my memory. Everyone in the Western world knows where they were when they heard the news of President Kennedy's assassination, or Princess Diana's death, but perhaps more indelibly etched in the memories of Mancunians is the event of 6 February, 1958. I remember dad coming home for tea (always at half past five) to inform us breathlessly that a plane carrying the Manchester United team had crashed after a European Cup tie, and there were many fatalities. United was, of course, the 'other' Manchester team and there was intense rivalry between local supporters. Feelings softened, however, when the whole of Manchester came together after the Munich air disaster, which claimed the lives of eight of the Manchester United team, and during the early sixties my friends and I would often drop in at Old Trafford of an evening to watch the legendary threesome, George Best, Bobby Charlton (one of the survivors of the crash) and Denis Law in action.

It seems strange now to think that a person's future life and career prospects could be forged at the age of eleven, but in 1957 I passed the eleven plus examination, and thus became one of the elite, a grammar school boy. This meant that I now had a very good chance of entering university in seven years time, which was not at all easy if this childhood test was failed.

Different cultures define the right of passage from childhood to manhood in various ways. Masai boys have to kill their first lion, but in 1950s Britain the transition from boyhood to young manhood was defined by the right to wear long, rather than short, trousers. My first impression of Ashton Grammar School was that it was populated by fellow pupils who were fully grown men and women and I had to get accustomed to being a lowly first former, or 'fag'.

Lessons were also more varied and sophisticated, to include French, Latin, and the Sciences. I now have a love of history, but my History teacher, Mr 'Screwy' Driver had a remarkable ability to make even the wonderfully rich, bloody, gory history of England seem incredibly dull. Probably because he himself was a very dull, humourless man, who also effectively ended my school sports career.

I was captain of the school's junior football team, and when playing other schools we were always supervised by a member of staff. Screwy had been assigned, I would think reluctantly, to look after the team on a Saturday morning match in nearby Oldham, and after the match caught me, and two other team members, sharing a Woodbine in the changing room! The outraged Screwy confiscated the offending cigarette and told us to report to the headmaster's office first thing Monday morning.

The headmaster, Mr Hopkinson, commanded the respect and fear of staff and students alike. He bore an uncanny resemblance to the present Conservative Foreign Secretary, William Hague, and if that was not frightening enough, he also had a formidable collection of canes. He was a burly man who played golf regularly, and loved to practise his swing using a suitable cane on the rear of miscreants of any size. So it was with some trepidation that I entered his study on that Monday morning, fully expecting 'The Wack' from one of those pieces of bamboo in my eye-line. However, as captain of the team I had to set an example, and smoking was an offence so grave that I was stripped of the captaincy and suspended from the team for an indefinite period. In fact I never played for the school again, although I continued as captain of the House team.

Screwy's uninspiring History lessons, did not, however, influence my drift away from the Arts into the Sciences. I had an enquiring mind, and always needed to know why. Why was the sky blue? Why was the sea salty? I cannot understand, even now, why non-scientist friends do not know the answers to these simple questions, and probably they do not even care. So at the end of 1961, well into my long-trouser phase, and armed with GCE O-levels in Physics, Chemistry, Biology, Mathematics, French and English language, there was no question that I would not stay on at school and study the sciences in the sixth form.

If, as the song says, school days are the happiest days of your life, then 1962 and 1963 have my fondest memories. Unencumbered with

French, Latin and Screwy's interminable History lessons, I could now concentrate on Physics, Chemistry and, less easily, Mathematics, and hone my leadership skills as a school prefect. I was also developing new interests. One of them was photography, and my cousin, Harry Butterworth, and I set up an informal partnership and entered business as professional photographers. 'Wilbut' did quite well, specialising in family portraits and weddings. My father, who after the war had taken a job as a van driver with the local newspaper, had now risen high enough in the hierarchy to pull a few strings, and I was able to spend my weekends as a sports photographer, travelling around the local football, rugby and cricket clubs, snapping team and action photographs. The only misfortune that arose was after one of our biggest wedding shoots. I was loading the films in my improvised darkroom, when dad entered and the light fogged everything. Informing the bride's parents wasn't the easiest job that I have ever had, and after the honeymoon, they and the invited guests had to dress up in their finery again for another, fixed-smiles, photo shoot. The darkroom this time was surrounded by guard-dogs and a high voltage security fence!

During these halcyon days I made some life-long friends. One of them, Eric Nield, introduced me to the local youth club, a plentiful source of my other new interest, girls. I loved the Albion Youth Club; there were pretty girls everywhere, we played badminton and listened to the new music from Merseyside. I spent virtually every night out, at the youth club, cinema and parties. Television did not play a great part in our lives, there were only two channels, but the boys would never leave the house on Friday nights until the end of 'Top of the Pops' which featured a leggy group of girls called 'Pan's People' who would dance very badly to the latest number one. I also vividly remember seeing on television the debut of a new band from Liverpool. The Beatles rapidly took the nation by storm, and they became lifetime favourites.

A neighbouring youth club visited our club in 1962, and one of the girls was a lovely blonde, who took a fancy to my friend Eric. Fortunately the relationship did not last long and she eventually became my first steady girlfriend. Little did I know that she would also become my wife, best friend and confidante, and my greatest support in all our travels around the world.

Partying in Ashton. Barbara and Barry are in the centre, with youth club friends (1963).

Barbara Atkinson also came from a very working class background. The eldest of six children, she had failed the eleven plus lottery and had attended the local girls' secondary modern school, before leaving to work in the centre of Manchester as a 'Hollerith', or 'punch-card' operator, providing the means of entering data into the early digital computers .

Barbara's father, Percy Atkinson, was, like my father, a southerner who had been drafted to the barracks in Ashton during the war, and also met and married a local girl, so I suppose that both Barbara and I had Adolf Hitler to thank for our very existence. Percy was a bus-conductor, and collected tickets on one of the local bus routes. One of his regular passengers was a shabbily dressed old man, who Percy befriended, and occasionally turned a blind eye to collecting his fare. The old man confided that he was a bit of an artist, and offered Percy one of his paintings, which he politely declined, as he did not wish to take anything in return for his kindness. Life's fortunes can be changed on such decisions; later it was discovered that the old man was one of Manchester's most famous sons, the artist L S Lowry, who died in 1976. His paintings of scenes of life in the industrial districts of northern England during the early twentieth century now sell for fortunes, his 'matchstick men' figures have often been criticised as being naïve, but a large collection of his work is on permanent public display in a purpose-built Salford Art Gallery appropriately named, The Lowry.

Barry Wills graduated from Leeds University with a PhD in Metallurgy and obtained a position on the Zambian copperbelt where he worked for four years. On his return to the UK he was appointed to a Senior Lectureship in Minerals Processing at the Camborne School of Mines in Cornwall. He is the author of Minerals Processing Technology and editor of the journal Minerals Engineering.

He lives in Falmouth with his wife, Barbara, and together with their son and daughter run Minerals Engineering International, organising conferences around the world.

JOHN JANSEN

John Jansen was born in Stanmore, Middlesex, in August 1946

I am a baby boomer, born in 1946. Although my birth certificate and passport say that I was born in Stanmore, Middlesex, my parents soon moved to Woodford Green, 'in Essex,' as my father always used to add. It later became part of the London Borough of Redbridge but my parents had escaped from the East End and regarded Essex as the countryside.

My earliest memory is associated with a visit to the group of shops known as the Broadway. I remember standing in the roadway trying to step up a very high kerbstone. My mother was some way ahead with my pushchair, looking back and waiting patiently. I remember looking up the hill at her. Our route passed a bowling green and I would look between the wooden railings of the gate and see the players in their whites bending down to bowl. Outside, parked at the curb, would be a number of cars, all black and upright with long, high bonnets. I would ask my mother to read the name badges to me. Our house was just over the brow of the hill so I was always aware of having to walk to the top and beyond to get home. The last shop was a sweet shop. My mother had a ration book with sugar coupons, which were used to buy sweets. I remember the actual occasion when rationing ended (I think sugar was the last rationing to go) and we went to buy sweets and surrender the book. The shop was very small with a recessed doorway, had a traditional bay window with small square panes of glass and a counter on the left as you went in, with long rows of jars of loose sweets. Across the back wall was a display of boxed sweets, mostly chocolates.

Another rationing incident I remember took place in the local Sainsbury's. This was a long, deep shop with a counter along each side from front to back (no supermarket shelves or self-service!). Across the back was a glass window into the office where you went to pay. All the sections, cheese, butter (where they weighed out the amount you wanted and then beat it into a block between two wooden paddles and hand wrapped it), and cooked meat had their own assistants. On one occasion we were nearly at the door when an assistant on the meat counter called out 'Mrs Jansen!' while waving her forgotten ration book in the air. She hurried back for it.

From our standpoint, the Central Line station cut off the Broadway from the shops beyond. I learned early on that the area on the other side of the tracks was not considered quite so good. The houses were older, smaller and mostly terraced and our cleaner, Mrs Jackson, lived there. She never stopped talking. We had a very long garden, which ran all the way down to the railway. Sometimes my mother would go right down the garden on some errand; when she got back Mrs Jackson would still be talking, not aware that mother had been out of the house. One reason to go down the garden was that for a while we had chickens. They had a proper house with laying boxes sticking out at the end. One lifted a flap like a piano lid to get the eggs. They had a run with a chicken wire fence. Sometimes the hens would try to fly away but I was told that their wings had been clipped. I remember one getting airborne after a fashion and crashing into a tree where it got all caught up. At some point rats were spotted coming up from the railway embankment and the chickens had to go. I was given the job of going to the butchers with two live hens in a wickerwork wheelie basket with the cloth lid tied on tight. I was probably about eight or nine then. I seem to remember that these returned as chickens for Sunday consumption. Other shops 'over the line' included the fish shop run by Mr Frost who lived next door. I was aware that he had a very upright, military bearing and spoke very well so that I was always rather shocked to see him in an apron serving wet fish 'over the line'.

One birthday I was given a Willies Jeep pedal car, which became my pride and joy. It was very detailed and had a miniature jerry can in a rack on the back. The windscreen could fold flat on the bonnet.

My father had laid flag stone paths around the garden as a roadway but this ended about two thirds of the way down and reverted to crazy paving which was much more difficult to drive on. There was nowhere to turn round so I had to get out and lift it round or back up. With a special kick of the pedals it would go backwards so I was quite experienced at this manoeuvre long before I drove a real car. I sometimes took it on the pavement outside and once went careering down the ramp in front of someone's drive, much to the consternation of a passing motorist. I was devastated when I finally outgrew it.

We lived in a semi-detached house, 42, Kings Avenue. Most family life took place in the kitchen and the living/dining room. The television would be on while we ate and it was unwise to speak, especially if dad was watching a quiz programme, at which he would be calling out the answers. It was somehow implicit that we (mother and I) showed admiration when he got them right, condemnation for the stupidity of the contestants when they got them wrong and outrage at how difficult they were when both dad and the contestant got them wrong. At least I remember feeling this as a youngster. When I got in from school but before dad got home, the kitchen was where mother and I would hang out. It was a large room and had a good sized table in the middle and a walk-in-pantry where I could usually find an apple tart or bread pudding. Provided some had already been cut, I could remove a portion with impunity. After dinner, in winter, dad would sit in an armchair pulled in front of the fire blocking the sight and warmth of it from us, smoking a cigarette and flicking his ash into the fireplace. At some stage we had a cat, which was once asleep on the hearth mat when a sudden heavy fall of soot took it by surprise.

I remember our first television, which was bought especially for the Coronation. It had a tall, floor-standing veneered cabinet with a small screen. I have heard that it was a pattern much repeated that the house in the street that had a television hosted everybody else for this event. I certainly remember the lounge at King's Avenue was packed for the occasion. Our next set, many years later was a quantum leap. It was a cuboid box which stood on a table, the screen was the entire front and the controls were on top under a spring loaded flap. At school I heard about the new ITV channel and programmes from other children, especially *Lassie*. We were behind the times on that one.

My primary school was St Anthony's. This Victorian building consisted of a long line of classrooms under one pitched roof. One simply entered the youngest class at one end (Mrs Lavery, once famously responded to while taking the register as Mrs Lavatory) and in time worked your way along the corridor. A skinny single lady who kept a greyhound with which she could have won an 'Owner and Dog Look-alike Competition' took the next class. I remember one occasion when she stood a naughty child in the corner facing the radiator. The child continued to be naughty and received a smack on the back of the head. His head went forward and he split his forehead open on the ornate ironwork. We all knew this was very bad! Next down the corridor came Sister Dolores' office. She was the Head and amazingly, a softy, unlike the Irish Sister Magdalen whose life work was to prove that the Inquisition was alive and kicking and the original inquisitors bungling amateurs. Before one got to her though, was Mrs Sayer's class. This had very high windows so that light could enter but not visual distractions. In spring, special shaped vases like milk bottles with a cup on top, were placed on the window sills with bulbs in them and the roots grew down towards us while the flowers were all but invisible. She used to get the school bus with the pupils as far as the Broadway, where she caught a train and so used to get off at the same stop as I did and would often give my mother an update. I was a very shy, reserved, goody-goody child but achieved what we would today call 'street cred' when she whacked me on the hands with her 'dolly', a stick a bit like a ruler, only for it to break. Having been much feared for as long as anybody could remember, its demise literally, at my hand, was greatly appreciated.

Mrs Sayer's class was separated from Sister Magdalen's by a wooden panelled partition. When the latter was in full cry, we who were destined to be in there the next year found it hard to concentrate. Whacking was used indiscriminately by both these teachers for behaviour and academic shortcomings so that though I could avoid one area of punishment, I was not immune. The good sister favoured a wooden classroom thermometer from which the glass was fortunately missing. When one was called to her desk for her to check your work book, her right hand and the piece of wood hovered just behind one's leg. Anything in the book which was deserving of criticism initiated a swift forward movement of hand and weapon.

One incident I have often told as it had such an impact on me. Behind the school was an unpaved lane, which was an alternate route to Woodford Green and my way home. There were a few cottages along this lane and a deep, water-filled ditch at one side. Once I was walking home this way with several others. One cottage was having some building work done and there was a pile of bricks outside. Somebody took a loose brick and threw it in the water. Several others joined in. Then an adult appeared and we all legged it. Next morning in Assembly, Sister Dolores read the riot act and demanded that the group owned up to her by break time. I was terrified, having never been in trouble and kept my head down but somebody told on me. I was summoned at lunch time, given the cane by Sister Dolores, and told that as an extra punishment for not having owned up, I was to go back and get the bricks out of the stream then and there, which I duly did. While engaged on this task, a man came out of the cottage and asked me what I was doing. I was pretty much scared of all authority figures, dad included, at that age. I could not admit to the truth. I said, 'Some naughty children from our school threw these bricks in the ditch and I volunteered to get them out.' The man was so impressed that he gave me half-a-crown. I think a Mars Bar was threepence at the time. Anyway, I bought all my newly acquired mates one on the way home. I never did find out who betrayed me.

John Jansen attended St Ignatius Grammar School in Tottenham. He spent six years in industry and then lived for a year in a kibbutz in Israel. On his return from Israel he attended Teacher Training College where he met his future wife, Lydia. John taught for thirteen years in state schools in Cheshire during which time he obtained an MSc by part-time study. In 1991 he was appointed Head of Design and Technology at Bedstone College in Shropshire where he later became Head of Studies. John and Lydia have a son, Luke, and a daughter, Ruth. They recently retired to Cornwall.

TIMELINE OF BRITISH SOCIAL HISTORY: 1951–1975

1951

Population reached 50·2 million. 25% of population was over the age of 50.

General Election won by Conservatives with Winston Churchill as PM.

Festival of Britain.

First UK supermarket opened by Express Dairies under the Premier Supermarkets brand in Streatham, London.

Prescription charges introduced for dental care and spectacles.

GCE O-level and A-level examinations introduced.

The Archers: start of regular 15 minute episodes whilst *The Goon Show* emerged from a pilot programme called *Crazy People* on BBC radio.

Zebra crossings introduced.

Nicholas Montserrat published *The Cruel Sea*.

1952

Death of King George V and accession of Elizabeth II.

Churchill announced that the UK has an atomic bomb, tested at the Monte Bello islands in Australia.

The De Havilland comet became the world's first jet airliner.

Disasters included the Lynmouth floods (34 killed) and the Harrow and Wealdstone train crash (108 deaths).

The Great Smog in London is believed to have killed 12,000

people immediately after the fog and a further 8,000 in the following months.

The Flower Pot Men introduced on children's television.

Evelyn Waugh published *Men at Arms,* Mary North published *The Borrowers* and E B White published *Charlotte's Web.*

The Mousetrap by Agatha Christie opened at the Ambassador's Theatre.

1953

James Watson and Francis Crick announced the discovery of the structure of the DNA molecule. The x-ray crystallographer Rosalind Franklin also played a vital role.

North Sea floods killed hundreds on the east coast.

The Samaritans telephone counselling service started by Chad Varah.

The first Cup Final on television in which Stanley Matthews helped Blackpool beat Bolton Wanderers 4–3. Stan Mortensen scored a hat trick for Blackpool.

Ian Fleming published *Casino Royale,* the first James Bond novel.

The first espresso coffee bar opened in London.

Laura Ashley sold her first printed fabrics.

Sweets and sugar rationing ended.

1954

UK Atomic Energy Authority founded.

Lord Montagu, Michael Pitt-Rivers and Peter Wildeblood were given prison sentences for homosexual activity.

Alan Turing (father of computer science) committed suicide following his conviction for gross indecency. The judge had offered him the choice between a prison sentence and chemical castration.

All rationing finally phased out after 14 years.

Kidbrooke School in Greenwich opened as Britain's first purpose-built comprehensive.

Roger Bannister became the first person to break the four minute mile.

Start of the radio comedy series *Hancock's Half Hour.*

J R R Tolkien published *The Lord of the Rings* and William Golding published *Lord of the Flies*.

First documented use of the term 'rock 'n' roll' coincided with 'Rock Around the Clock' recorded by Bill Haley and His Comets and Elvis Presley's first commercial recording 'That's All Right Mama'.

1955

General Election won by the Conservatives with Anthony Eden becoming PM.

Hugh Gaitskell became leader of the Labour Party.

American virologist Dr Jonas Salk promoted a polio vaccine in Britain.

Ruth Ellis became the last woman to be hanged in the UK.

ITV began broadcasting the first commercial television.

Stirling Moss became the first English winner of the British Grand Prix.

The film *The Dam Busters* was released.

Lonnie Donnegan recorded 'Rock Island Line'.

Airfix produced their first scale model aircraft kit, a Supermarine Spitfire.

1956

Suez Crisis. President Nasser of Egypt nationalised the Suez Canal in response to US and UK withdrawal of funds for the Aswan Dam Project. In November British and French paratroopers were involved in an invasion of Egypt but withdrew under intense American pressure.

Hungarian Revolution was brutally suppressed by Russian troops. 250,000 Hungarians left the country with many coming to the UK (October).

Clean Air Act (1956) passed by Parliament in response to the Great London Smog.

First large-scale trials of contraceptive pill.

The hard disc drive invented by an IBM team.

The Queen opened the first two 65 megawatt dual purpose nuclear reactors at Windscale (Sellafield).

Jim Laker set a record at Old Trafford in the fourth test between

England and Australia by taking 19 wickets in a first class match.

John Osborne's play *Look Back in Anger* opened at the Royal Court theatre in London.

Elvis Presley entered the US charts with 'Heartbreak Hotel'.

1957

Anthony Eden resigned as PM citing ill health and was replaced by Harold Macmillan. Macmillan was later to tell party members in Bedford that 'most of our people have never had it so good'.

World's first nuclear plant accident at Windscale. Details of the accident were suppressed by the government for 30 years.

Britain tested its first hydrogen bomb at Maiden Island in the Pacific.

USSR launched the satellite Sputnik, the dawn of global telecommunications

The Wolfenden Report recommended that 'homosexual behaviour between consenting adults in private should not be considered a criminal offence'.

Lewisham train crash in which 90 people died and 173 were injured.

Andy Capp first appeared as cartoon character in the *Daily Mirror*.

Release of David Lean's film *The Bridge on the River Kwai*.

John Braine published *Room at the Top* and Lawrence Durrell published *Justine* the first of the Alexandrian Quartet.

1958

Bertrand Russell launched the Campaign for Nuclear Disarmanent (CND), which held the first march from Aldermaston in protest against nuclear weapons.

Ian Donald published an article in the *Lancet* explaining the diagnostic use of ultrasound.

An exhibition of computers held at Earls Court: the first of its kind.

The Duke of Edinburgh's Award presented for the first time.

Donald Campbell broke the water speed record at 248·62 mph.

4.5 million cars on the road: 5,970 people killed in road accidents.

The opening of the Preston bypass: the first stretch of motorway (M6).

The first broadcast of the long-running children's television programme *Blue Peter*.

Premiere of *Carry on Sergeant*: the first of the 'Carry On' films.

Cliff Richard's debut single 'Move It' reached number two in the charts.

1959

General Election won by the Conservative Party with Harold Macmillan as PM.

Margaret Thatcher entered Parliament as MP for Finchley.

The first post codes were introduced.

The first section of the M1 was opened between Watford and Rugby.

Launch of the Bush TR82 transistor radio.

Iona and Peter Opie published *The Lore and Language of Schoolchildren*.

The first of the *Ivor the Engine* series on children's television.

1960

Conscription ended as the last man was called up for National Service.

First televised Royal Wedding as Princess Margaret married Antony Armstong-Jones.

The Queen launched the first British nuclear submarine.

Penguin Books found not guilty of obscenity in publishing *Lady Chatterley's Lover*. 200,000 copies of the book sold in one day.

Michael Woodruff performed the first successful kidney transplant in the UK.

First episode of *Coronation Street* on television.

Launch of the film *Saturday Night and Sunday Morning*.

1961

Population reached 52.8 million.

Amnesty International formed as a consequence of Peter Benensen's newspaper article 'The Forgotten Prisoners'.

Birth control pills became available on the NHS.

Betting shops were legalised.

Launch of the iconic E-type Jaguar.

The Beatles performed at the Cavern Club for the first time.

Acker Bilk's 'Stranger on the Shore' released.

Tottenham Hotspur became the first team in the century to win both the League and FA Cup.

1962

Harold Macmillan dismissed 13 cabinet ministers in the 'Night of the Long Knives'.

James Hanratty hanged at Bedford Prison for the A6 murder, in spite of many people believing in his innocence.

Race riots in Dudley, West Midlands.

Release of *Dr No:* the first James Bond film.

First episode of the satirical show *That Was the Week That Was.*

Release of David Lean's film *Lawrence of Arabia.*

1963

Harold Macmillan resigned as PM and was succeeded by Alec Douglas Home.

Hugh Gaitskell died suddenly and was succeeded by Harold Wilson as leader of the Labour Party.

Charles De Gaulle vetoed British entry into the EEC.

John Profumo resigned as Secretary of State for War over his affair with Christine Keeler.

The Great Train Robbery took place in Buckinghamshire.

Dr Beeching issued a report calling for huge cuts to the UK rail network.

The Robbins Report, recommending the immediate expansion of universities, was accepted by the Government.

Douglas Engelbart invented the computer mouse.

First episode of *Dr Who* screened on television.

1964

General Election won by the Labour Party with a majority of five: Harold Wilson became PM.

The last executions in Britain took place: Peter Allen and Gwynne Evans.

The House of Commons voted to abolish capital punishment.

Helen Brook opened the first centre to provide teenage contraception and sexual health advice.

The Sun newspaper went into circulation.

1965

Edward Heath became leader of the Conservative Party.

The Race Relations Act outlawed public racial discrimination.

Infant mortality rate averaged 20 deaths per 1,000 live births.

The Ministry of Education issued a circular requesting Local Authorities to convert their schools to the comprehensive system.

The Certificate of Secondary Education (CSE) introduced as a school-leaving qualification.

Introduction of the 70 miles per hour speed restriction on motorways.

Mary Quant introduced the miniskirt.

The Rolling Stones released 'The Last Time' and 'I Can't Get No Satisfaction'.

1966

General Election won by the Labour Party under Harold Wilson. His majority increased from one to 96.

Aberfan disaster in South Wales caused by the collapse of a coal spoil tip. 144 people were killed, including 116 children.

Barclays Bank introduced the first British credit card.

Construction began on first AGR reactor in UK and a prototype Fast Breeder reactor opened at Dounreay.

England won the World Cup, beating West Germany 4–2. The game attracted an all-time record television audience of 32 million.

The existing motorways M1, M4 and M6 were expanded.

The Beatles released their album *Revolver* and their single 'Paperback

Writer' reached number one in the charts.

1967
Parliament de-criminalised homosexuality.
Parliament legalised abortion on a number of grounds.
The first North Sea gas pumped ashore.
The first scheduled colour television broadcasts began with a coverage of Wimbledon.
The Beatles released *Sergeant Pepper's Lonely Hearts Club Band*.

1968
The Theatre Act ended censorship of the theatre.
Enoch Powell made his controversial 'Rivers of Blood' speech and was dismissed from the Shadow cabinet.
Introduction of 5 and 10 pence coins in the run-up to decimalisation.
Completion of the M1 motorway.
First performance of the Andrew Lloyd Webber and Tim Rice musical *Joseph and the Amazing Technicolor Dreamcoat*.

1969
American astronauts landed on the moon: 'a small step for man, a giant leap for mankind'.
Representation of the People Act lowered the voting age from 21 to 18.
Introduction of the new 50 pence coin, which replaced the 10 shilling note.
The Beatles released *Abbey Road*, their last album recorded together.
Ken Loach's film *Kes* released.
The first appearance of *The Clangers* on children's television.
The space hopper toy introduced to Britain.
Eric Carle published *The Very Hungry Caterpillar*.

1970
General Election won by the Conservatives under Ted Heath with

a majority of 30.

A Boeing 747 landed at Heathrow airport: the first jumbo jet to land in Britain.

BP discovered a large oil field in the North Sea.

55% of men and 44% of women were cigarette smokers.

The first Glastonbury Festival took place.

Andrew Lloyd Webber and Tim Rice released the album *Jesus Christ Superstar*.

The last forced child migration to Australia.

The 10 shilling note withdrawn from circulation.

English translation published of Gabriel Garcia Marquez's novel *One Hundred Years of Solitude*.

1971

Population reached 55.9 million.

Owner-occupation of property reached 50%.

The BBC Open University opened.

The House of Commons voted in favour of joining the EEC.

Divorce Reform Act came into effect allowing couples to divorce after a separation of two years. The number of divorces in the UK exceeded 100,000 for the first time.

Average family size decreased to two children per family.

Ibrox disaster: 66 people killed on a stairway crush at a Celtic v Rangers match in Glasgow.

The Angry Brigade bombed the house of Robert Carr, Secretary of State for Employment.

The UK switched to decimal currency.

The anti-smoking pressure group ASH formed.

E-mail invented by Roy Tomlinson.

Roger Hargreaves published *Mr Tickle:* the first in the 'Mr Men' series.

The term 'motorway madness' used by police describing Britain's worst road accident in foggy conditions on the M6 near Warrington.

1972

Unemployment exceeded a million for the first time since the 1930s.

50,000 Ugandan Asians expelled by Idi Amin with many coming to the UK.

BEA flight 548 crashed killing all 118 people on board: the worst UK air disaster.

School leaving age raised to 16.

First public demonstration of ARPANET (forerunner of internet) using 40 machines.

Mastermind first screened on television.

Richard Adams published *Watership Down.*

1973

UK entered the EEC.

VAT came into effect at a rate of 10% as a consequence of EEC membership.

The British Library was established.

Emmerdale: one of the longest running soaps first screened on television.

The Three Day Week introduced by the Conservatives at midnight on 31 December, 1973, as a measure to conserve electricity during the strike by coal miners.

First international connection to internet between University College, London and the Royal Radar Establishment in Norway.

1974

Two general elections took place. The first election, held in February, resulted in a hung parliament with the Labour Party forming a minority government. In October a second election resulted in the Labour Government having a majority of three under Harold Wilson.

The IRA carried out an extensive programme of bombing in England, which included the Houses of Parliament and the home of former PM Edward Heath.

Inflation soared to 17·2%.

Emo Rubik, Hungarian sculptor and professor of architecture, invented the Rubik cube. It became the world's top-selling puzzle game.

Mcdonalds opened their first restaurant in Woolwich, London.

First appearance of *Bagpuss* on children's television.
Art Fry and Spencer Silver invented 'Post-it' notes.

1975
Margaret Thatcher defeated Edward Heath to become leader of the Conservative Party.

67% of voters supported continued membership of the EEC in a referendum.

Inflation reached 24.2%: the second highest since records began.

Altair produced the first portable computer

32 people killed in a coach crash in West Yorkshire: the highest toll in a UK road accident.

First episode of the comedy *Fawlty Towers* on television.

Angela Rippen became the first female to present the national television news.

First series of the children's television request programme *Jim'll Fix It*, fronted by former disc jockey Jimmy Savile.

STEPHEN LAY

Stephen Lay was born in Redruth, Cornwall, in June 1955

I was the eldest of four children, brought up in a small Cornish village named Praze-an-Beeble (Cornish for 'river through the field') between Camborne and Helston. Little did I know during my childhood that my immediate environment and the Camborne School of Mines, just three miles away, would shape my life.

Praze is at the junction of two roads with a 'Square' and a 'Plan' (plantation). The village grew around the local mining industry, agriculture and as service housing to the local mansion. It had a railway station, boasts a fine cricket field and a primary school.

From the time I was born through to 1963 we lived at 78, Fore Street, which was in the Square and just opposite the St Aubyn Arms and the post office. Our house was a large double-fronted terrace house, it had to be, everybody knew where our door was. Fore Street is the main street leading uphill to Camborne and has terraced housing on both sides with the occasional alley between which was usually built over. There are no front gardens. The front doors open on to the street. The terraces were interrupted only by the two Methodist chapels. There were two shops: Tishaw's and Glasson's which sold everything. In those days we bought potatoes by the gallon (weighing ten pound I seem to remember). On more than one occasion my father described Mr Tishaw, in a rather derogatory way, as 'a do-gooder'; as a young child who was always being told to be good that statement stuck in my mind as being very strange, what could be wrong with doing good? Many years later I realised that Mr Tishaw was a Freemason, an organisation that my father greatly disliked.

The Baigents sold newspapers and ran the fish and chip shop (down another alley). Mr Rosemurgy was the cobbler. The back gardens on both sides of Fore Street were long. A herd of cows was kept in one, or is this something I have imagined? Our neighbour, at number 80, was Mr Coleman who was the local service agent for Singer sewing machines; I recall that it was not until the early 1960s that he installed a bathroom, I'm not sure what they did before. We had one.

My father's parents were of Cornish descent and lived at the top of Fore Street, 'Lisvean' (number seven) and above almost everybody else (well my grandmother thought she was!). Lisvean appears to be two double-fronted terraced houses separated by an arched alley but joined by bedrooms above. The entrance to the alley had large arched doors, with a domestic size door set into them, these opened straight on to the street. I was led to believe that in 'olden times' the horse and carriage pulled in here and went through to the stables and to the servants quarters at the back, very plausible. From the road there were a couple of steps down to the granite flagstones. How did the horse and carriage cope with that? Then followed a couple of steps up on the right to the dining room. In this door was a glazed panel with a date scratched in the glass. I was told that it had been scratched with a diamond and the date was that of the Great Blizzard of March 1891. What excitement: a diamond and a blizzard. Every winter we longed for snow! The door on the left went into the drawing room where there was a piano and, over the fireplace, a (tacky) framed picture of angels and clouds. I spent many hours looking at that picture wondering what on earth it was all about. The drawing room led also to another hallway, to my grandfather's office, to a library and another flight of stairs. All very posh, too posh to worship at the Methodist churches. It had to be at the parish church at Crowan. Yet my grandmother insisted she always voted for Labour; I could never understand that.

The road to Helston (and to Praze station and to Clowance estate) was Station Hill, which had newer houses with front gardens. These backed on to the cricket field. The railway line skirted Clowance estate and the cricket field, I recall the steam engines plying between Helston and the main line junction at Gwinear Road. Just beyond the bridge over Station Road the line was protected by a hardly visible Second World War pill box set into the embankment. We never did work out how to get into it despite hours of planning!

The village abuts the Clowance estate, once the seat to the St Aubyn family, but in my childhood it was owned by Mr Glanville, who lived in a few rooms of the decaying mansion. The extensive estate and gardens were overgrown and irresistible to adventurous youngsters. My mother's parents were tenants at properties on the estate. Pheasant Cottage had no electricity and relied on bottled gas for lighting; the lavatory was down the garden. I clearly remember the gas mantle lights being lit; the occasional gas bottle flash-back; the cold water for washing and the rats. The cottage was enclosed by a high wall. On two sides it backed on to Clowance nursery which was a total 'no go' area. I recall expeditions with my father to try and establish what was over the wall, but it was not until I was in my teens that we became friends of the new owner and became regular visitors. Until then what was behind those enormously high (to a six-year-old) walls remained a complete mystery and the source of many nightmares. At another time my grandparents lived in one of the wings of the estate's old stables. This was a remote, dark building shrouded by colossal trees and rhododendrons. It comprised two wings and a clock tower, all locked and inaccessible. Again, imagine the fear of a child staying at this remote and ghostly place. But Clowance holds many pleasant memories of picking primroses in the spring and blackberries in the autumn, foraging for chestnuts and picking holly with berries. Today many thousands will know Clowance as a timeshare holiday resort. Pheasant Cottage is still there and the stables and clock tower are now luxurious apartments.

The Square was more than a square. It had a quite large area of grass surrounded by tall trees and 'the Plan' (from 'plantation'). The Plan is separated from the road by granite posts with a low slung, heavy iron chain; it has a war memorial and swings and was where the youth of the village congregated and played. It was the centre of activities during Praze Fair Week, the first week of July when the chains were removed and the Anderson and Rowlands fair took up residence with dodgems, roundabouts and various stalls. On the Saturday children and adults danced the Flora dance. The dance originated in Helston but was later sacrilegiously immortalised by Terry Wogan's 'The Floral Dance'. The dance made its way from the Square up and down Station Hill and Fore Street and was led by local dignitaries. We all looked forward to the fair coming to Praze, it was a great family affair. But one year Mr Hosken dropped dead at the end of the dance and as a consequence my father did not come to the fair with me. I was very disappointed. Praze Fair week also featured an agricultural show and a carnival.

We attended Sunday school at Crowan church, irregularly, but were sure to be there for prize-giving! The Methodists organised

Stephen and his brother with Red Indian feathers.

their annual tea-treats when a double-decker bus would pick us all up from the Square and take us and our families to the beach at Carbis Bay, where we would be treated to a large saffron bun. Today these are still sold in the local bakeries as 'tea-treat buns'. I wonder how many know why they are called that?

The other roads running from the square are the Leedstown road with only Bourdeaux's Bakery, famous throughout the area for their Cornish pasties. Opposite was Leslie Blewett's house and workshops, he was the village carpenter and undertaker. In a cellar was the chapel of rest, another scary place.

Then there is School Road which in places had the River Beeble, no more than a stream, running alongside. It was about a quarter of a mile walk for us from 78, Fore Street to Crowan Church of England Primary School. This was quite a grand building as it had been rebuilt a few years before following a fire. There were three classrooms, a hall, a large playground and outside toilets (sorry, 'lavatories') and a kitchen as most of us had school dinners. My first teacher was a kindly Mrs Keoghan who lived in Helston, followed by a spinster, Miss Lawrence, who lived at the top of Fore Street. 'Pasty' Williams who was the head teacher, I think he came from St Austell. I still remember my first day at school. A quarter of a mile was a long way for a young child. I had strict instructions from my 'posh' grandmother to do everything I was told. In assembly I had a real problem as I was being told to 'lift up your hearts', but how did I do that? I stood on tip toe! I loved sports but apart from Sports Day held at the cricket field that was the only sport we did, apart from 'music and mime'.

On the way to primary school we would pass the blacksmith who made a living in a hovel of a building, and then a small car mechanics in a dilapidated small shed. Just before we reached the council estate was a small overgrown enclosure, which I understood to have been the school garden, another place of intrigue.

For Praze children, secondary school was likely to be in Camborne as very few passed the eleven plus exam and went to grammar school. Those who did usually went to Redruth or Truro by bus or to Helston by train. In 1966, the headmaster of Helston Grammar came to Crowan Primary to interview me. I was the only one to go to grammar school that year, not by train, but by bus as Dr Beeching had axed our branch line.

There was no doctor in Praze until 1952 when my father set up his GP practice in the face of opposition from the Camborne practices. The front two rooms were a waiting room and a surgery. My most dominant childhood memories are the telephone ringing and my father shouting, 'Next please!' towards the waiting room. My mother looked after all the administrative side of the practice. Every waking hour revolved around the practice. Surgery from nine o'clock in the morning for an 'hour' but it often went on far longer; house visits through the day; evening surgery from six in the evening (or was it seven?) until late. It was not often we would see our father in the evenings. Apart from the occasional locum there was no relief until an agreement was made with Dr Dean at Porthleven: they would cover for each other on alternate weekends. The phone was the bane of our lives; every time it rang 'Praze three-eight-six, Dr Lay's surgery' meant business and often a visit regardless of weather, time of night or seriousness of the patient's condition. It seemed that the phone tied us to the house all of the time. I'm told now that when dad had his weekend off the postmistress or operator would connect all Praze three-eight-six calls to Dr Dean (those were the days when there was a switchboard with wires and plugs). But I clearly remember staying at Pheasant Cottage half a mile away and being woken in the middle of the night to return to 78, Fore Street because mum could hear the phone and it had to be answered! Often my parents' dedication to others was rewarded by gifts from patients. In those days chicken was a special treat. On more than one occasion we were brought a chicken, still alive awaiting a fate (worse than death?) at the hands of my father who never did master dispatching chickens quickly. To supplement our diet our parents bred rabbits for food.

Dad liked his cars; my earliest memories are of a car with running boards but we also had a Jowett Javelin and a couple of Mark One Jaguars. At some time my father bought a circa 1940s Trojan Brooke Bond Tea van and converted it into a camper van complete with bunk beds and a swing down table. Overnight expeditions were made to Gwithian beach and to Lestowder at the mouth of the Helford River. Getting there in an exhaust-filled misfiring vintage vehicle was the challenge. Fifty years on and now three Lay generations continue to enjoy camping at Lestowder, though the Trojan is no more.

Employment was not a problem in Praze during my childhood. I would be woken at about a quarter to seven each morning as our neighbours' cars spluttered to life and revved up Fore Street towards Camborne. I would lie in bed listening to each imagining how far they got before out of ear shot, as far as PC Glasson's police house opposite the chapel at the top of Fore Street? Their destinations were many: the mines, Holmans Brothers Engineering works at Camborne or Nancekuke top-secret nerve gas works. Nobody knew what happened at Nancekuke, none of my school friends whose fathers worked there knew. Even today it remains a mystery. Holmans were the major employer serving the international mining industry. In those days a very real option instead of O-levels or GCEs was an apprenticeship at Holmans.

The local tin and copper mine dumps along the Helston Road at Horse Downs were another haunt for us: exploring the dumps, throwing stones down the mine shafts and counting until they hit water, collecting mineral specimens, spotting adders and picking wild strawberries that thrived on the barren ground. In the early 1960s there was renewed interest in tin exploration. I clearly remember visiting diamond drill rigs and being fascinated by what riches still lay below our feet despite centuries of mining heritage.

In 1963 the family moved to Moorfield, immediately behind the school. The surgery moved there as well. In the mid 1980s my father retired, but the practice continued at Moorfield until an alternative could be found. In 2010 my mother and our daughter, Dr Tamsin Lay also a GP, were asked to open the new purpose-built Praze Surgery. In sixty years Praze Surgery had moved no further than two hundred and fifty yards from its original location and had grown by thousands of patients. What goes round comes around?

Stephen Lay failed most of his A-levels but was accepted on to a diploma course at the nearby Camborne School of Mines. Discovering a motivating environment he eventually graduated with a BSc (Hons) in Mining Engineering. In his final year he married Carol, purchased and renovated his first house and was President of the Students Association. After graduation he obtained employment at South Crofty tin mine, working his way up the ladder. After being made redundant in 1991 he became a consultant mining engineer and has worked in many countries. 'I never looked back!'

Stephen and Carol have two daughters, Tamsin and Naomi and a son, Ian.

CAROL LAY

*Carol Lay (née Thomas) was born in
Chorlton-cum-Hardy, Manchester, in January 1954*

I was born at 27, Torbay Road, Chorlton-cum-Hardy, where I lived for three years with my mother, Cornish father and nana, my maternal grandmother. Whilst there my mother returned to work as a nursery nurse and dad looked after me with some help from nana. On one occasion I fell down the backdoor steps, cut my upper lip on the metal mop bucket and have lived with the scar ever since: a living memory!

In 1957 we all moved to Cornwall to a cottage in Perranuthnoe. This was to enable my dad to obtain work as an agricultural mechanic, which sometimes involved him travelling to the Isles of Scilly. We only lived in Perranuthnoe for a very short time. The cottage was called 'The Rosary'. It was a tied farm worker's cottage where my uncle should have lived, but as he was unmarried and still lived with his parents, we were able to stay there. We were there for about four months before moving a mile inland to the village of Goldsithney to another rented cottage. At the same time nana moved to her own rented secluded cottage down Gears Lane. It was at the bottom of an unmade lane without electricity, gas or running water indoors. Meanwhile, at our place, 3, Retallack Cottages, we did have electricity and running cold water but no bathroom, the Elsan toilet was at the bottom of the garden. Nana's toilet was also an Elsan and she obtained her water by bucket from a galvanised tank which collected rainwater. Lucky dad got the job of emptying both toilets.

Goldsithney was quite a big village in comparison with Perranuthnoe. It boasted two pubs, the Crown and the Trevelyan

Arms. There were two shops when we first moved there. Jordan's was a small shop run by Mrs Jordan and her daughter where they sold the bare essentials. I remember the big scales and the weights for selling potatoes but most of all I remember the jars of sweets. My favourites were Murray Mints. Mrs Jordan could always be relied upon to serve you from the side door when they were closed if your mother sent you for an emergency packet of chocolate biscuits for unexpected visitors. Then there was Hosking's, a family grocers. They were a proper shop, having specific counters for different things such as bacon and cream. Once I was old enough it was my job to take mum's weekly order up to Hosking's on a Friday morning and the order was duly delivered to our door on Friday afternoon. Eventually, by the time I was nine or ten another shop opened in Goldsithney. This was run by a family from 'Up North' called the Boultons and their shop included a butcher's and greengrocer's. Mum would buy her fruit and vegetables from Mr Boulton when he came around in his van and give him the meat order which was collected on a Saturday.

Goldsithney also boasted a garage, a post office, a Methodist chapel, a builders and undertakers, a primary school and Miss Mary. Miss Mary delivered the newspapers. She had a surname, Yglesias, but it was 'foreign' so she stuck to using her Christian name. She was quite a character, very rotund with a mop of grey curls, always wearing khaki dungaree type trousers and thick jumpers. She lived in a very run down cottage, kept hordes of cats and was mad about all animals. Woe betide you if she caught you standing on a snail or pulling a worm to pieces, which of course I never did! Her sister opened and ran the bird sanctuary at Mousehole. Miss Mary was always considered a bit eccentric but I don't think she ever did anybody any harm; looking back she was probably quite lonely.

Shortly after moving to Goldsithney my brother Nigel was born. It was a home birth, which was the norm then. I remember waiting on the landing to go in and see him but can't remember more than that. Nigel and I both went to the village school where Miss Mayes taught us. The school was quite small. You went in through the cloakroom where the named coat hooks were situated. There were sinks at one end and a door leading to the playground, sports field and the toilets.

Carol in school uniform with brother Nigel in the garden
at 3, Retallack Cottages, in Goldsithney (1961).

The door to the classroom led off from the cloakroom as well. It was a typical classroom with windows set up high in the wall, letting in plenty of light but too high for you to see through and get distracted. It was heated by a big stove at the front and there was a huge fire guard all the way around it. Miss Mayes had her desk adjacent to the stove and we all sat in rows looking towards the front. There were between twenty and thirty of us from the ages of five to eleven and we were streamed by age working from 'seeds' through to 'buds' and finally 'flowers'. Miss Mayes did everything and the only help she had was a dinner lady, although there were no hot dinners while I was there. Children either took packed lunch or went home for lunch. I went home as we only lived around the corner. I remember us all sitting on the carpet sewing running stitches through Binca. Miss Mayes sat above us all tying knots and re-threading needles.

I only made it as far as the 'buds' because my parents and a group of about five others decided the school wasn't doing very well and that Miss Mayes had her favourites, usually from well-to-do families such as farmers and doctors. Whatever the reason, when I was six years old we left Goldsithney school and moved to St Mary's Church of England school in Penzance, which was five miles from the village. It was a very religious school with Father Sargeson taking assembly a couple of times a week and very regular excursions to St Mary's Church in Chapel Street for services throughout the year. St Mary's was 'high church' and girls regularly fainted because of the swinging incense. Looking back I have St Mary's to thank for being able to recite verbatim the nine lessons read at carol services.

There were two tuck shops near school. One was right outside the school gates and the other beside the afternoon bus stop. The shop near school was called Mann's Dairy. My grandad worked for Primrose Dairy and part of his round sometimes included Mann's. If he spotted me through the railings in the playground it usually meant extra tuck money. I usually had one penny a day. Sometimes I bought biscuits at playtime: for one penny you could get two Rich Teas or one chocolate digestive.

I took my eleven plus and had an interview. I didn't pass: it was probably a good thing. At Heamoor Secondary School I was always at the top of the class and did well, I don't think I would have much liked being at, or near, the bottom, which I probably would have been at the grammar school.

Despite going to a Church of England school I was brought up as a Methodist. Goldsithney Chapel was very much central to our daily and social lives. My dad was a steward at the chapel. My brother and I went to Sunday school at a quarter past ten, then into chapel at eleven o'clock and returned to Sunday school part way through the service until it had finished. When we were old enough we were allowed to stay in chapel for the sermon, which usually lasted at least twenty minutes. Then there was 'Sunshine Corner' on a Wednesday evening. Sisters Joyce and Judith, both deaconesses, taught us about religion and the Bible through fun activities and singing choruses. One of my favourites was 'Climb, climb up sunshine mountain'! I can still remember most of the songs we learnt. I also went to Youth Fellowship once I was thirteen. It was a sort of religious Young Farmers where many amongst them met their partners. We sang a lot, took services as a group and generally had a great deal of fun.

We lived at Retallack Cottages until I was about eight. It was quite a big cottage where we washed in the scullery. Mum had some sort of boiler which she used to heat the water for the washing and then on Saturday evenings it was put on again to heat up water for bath night. Dad brought in the tin bath and put it in front of the Rayburn.

Our next move was to 21, South Road, a two-bedroomed council house around the corner where I shared a bedroom with my brother. We had a back garden where dad grew vegetables and a front garden with grass and a few roses. But the luxury was that here we had running hot and cold water and a bathroom and inside toilet. Many of my friends were already living on the estate where I became known as 'Miss Prim' because I wore my cardigan over my shoulders and I wasn't allowed to play out on a Sunday. Dad was very strict about what you could and couldn't do on Sunday: no eating ice cream or going to the beach were some of the rules. We used to go out for walks as a family, or out for a drive and every other Sunday we had tea at my grandma and grandad's. Dad's brothers and their families went as well. Grandma used to bake almost everything we had from the fatless sponges to the splits (soft bread rolls). She even made the clotted cream using milk from her sister's dairy herd.

Dad always found time to spend with us, he read my bedtime story and listened to my prayers. He taught me to tie my laces and years later to drive, telling me to leave the hedge trimming to the Council, and ultimately passing on his love of roses to me.

Nana lived down Gears Lane for about ten years. She did eventually get electricity but never running water or an inside toilet, so it was always boiled water and strip washes. She kept her Rayburn going summer and winter and there was always a 'guzunder' at night. Nana's entertainment and company was a radio she rented from Radio Rentals. She introduced me to *The Archers* and *Friday Night is Music Night* which was also a signal that it was time for me to go to bed. The lane never improved all the time she lived there but now it has tarmac and has street lights as there are several housing estates there. Eventually she moved to a purpose built old people's bungalow where she luxuriated with 'all mod cons' plus a view of the Isles of Scilly in good weather.

My memories are good ones: Saturday afternoons shopping in Penzance with mum and nana, enjoying orange squash and fancies in Warren's café, and family holidays. Each summer we went to Manchester to stay with Auntie Edith and Uncle Jack, travelling there in a hired turquoise Ford Anglia. The journey took all day. Mum packed bacon sandwiches for breakfast, which we ate on Bodmin Moor. Later we stopped for more sandwiches under the Clifton Suspension Bridge. I was always travel sick and took Kwells with a spoonful of jam, but could be guaranteed to be sick before we even reached Relubbas, a mere three miles up the road. To this day I cannot bear eating jam from a spoon!

Carol Lay attended a Teacher Training College in Hertfordshire. She started to specialise in special education three days after her marriage to Stephen in 1976. Carol has carried out outstanding work within the field of special education in Cornwall throughout her career and gained an MEd and headship qualification on the way. She retired from education in 2005 and is now busy with family and voluntary work.

'We have three fantastic children and an extended family in whom we delight. I have had a great life and I am who I am because of life's rich tapestry'.

BARRY AUSTIN

Barry Austin was born in Hagley, Worcestershire, in June 1954

In the 1950s Hagley seemed like the village where 'the wooden-tops' lived. We even had a spotty dog and a picket fence. Though it was, even then, a commuter village for the Black Country with all its foundries, it still seemed rural, with a clarity of silence that has now disappeared. There was a railway station, shops and pubs, maybe two thousand people in all. Our biggest claim to fame was when the Queen visited on St George's Day, 23 April, 1957. It was really the starting point of a Royal Tour of the West Midlands, which included Halesowen, Stourbridge and Kidderminster, so she just got off the train at Hagley.

In my early years it always seemed to be summer, except when there was snow! That in itself indicates how impressions can shape one's memories, and I was lucky as my memories are warm; a loving family and a happy primary school life. It was a small school, everyone knew everyone, and teachers were quirky, no OFSTED then. The headteacher, or headmaster as was the term then, used to have favourites. I was one such favourite, and I would be asked to come to the front of the class, where I would sit in a chair facing the rest of the class. He would ask questions and if I got one right I'd get a penny. No one got a penny unless they were a favourite, so whilst it boosted my pocket money I don't recall it making me many friends.

Children can be cruel. I recall a gypsy girl coming to the school who had an aroma that was noticeable. The children chased her round the coal bunkers shouting 'smelly-stinker' and, though I wasn't happy with it I wasn't strong or old enough to make a stand, so watched helplessly as she ran and ran till she burst into tears and fell on the ground. I still feel a sense of guilt.

Heather Matthews went to the school, she was a bit younger than me and she was beautiful, and I loved her. I don't recall her personality, but that didn't matter to a love-struck nine-year-old. I knew even then you couldn't have everything, so I settled to love someone who was beautiful. That love was not reciprocated. I had plenty of time to dwell on her as, from the age of seven, I walked the mile or so to school. I remember 'flying' over the pavement and my feet had to avoid all cracks, or I would die a hideous death. I never managed to make it to school without treading on a crack, but never did meet the dreadful end I imagined. I do remember being told that if I stuck my tongue out at a weathercock it would remain stuck, and I recall passing it in fear of accidentally showing a small part of my tongue!

We lived in a detached house that my dad, an architect, had designed. It was on the edge of the village, overlooking fields and woods. I shared a room with two brothers and had the top bunk. From there I could watch the sun setting over the pine woods, a beautiful view and enhanced as I listened to the BBC news on my crystal-set radio, with its one ear piece. I can't remember any news, but I remember a sense of how big the world was; all that news of other people in other places. Occasionally I would hear an aeroplane overhead at night and used to lie there and imagine all those people sitting in their seats, people I didn't know, flying to places I had never been to.

We lived on an avenue, right in the middle, but isolated as few other houses had then been built. We had fields either side. Nice fields, with tall grass, indeed dry grass; grass that, when lit with a match (by my older brother) flared into sheets of flame. Unfortunately, following a dry spell, these sheets of flame defied all attempts at being put out and so the fire brigade was called out to stop the fire spreading to fields and hedges beyond. Mum was in bed, with a threatened miscarriage, unbeknown to us, and shortly after lost twin babies. Girls. She already had three boys and wanted a girl. We didn't care about girls, but I often wonder now if the two incidents were related. Soon after she became pregnant again, but had another boy. Even now we find it in our hearts to occasionally remind him about being 'the girl mum always wanted'.

Cars, they smelt right in the 1950s. A mixture of leather, mildew, petrol, and something else that defies description. Grandma had an early Morris Minor; we loved to travel with her as it had yellow 'flipper' indicators that would rise to the horizontal when the strange white knob on the dashboard was twisted left or right. If we were good we would be allowed to twist if for her. Not encumbered by safety belts we would have two or three small boys on the front seat, all vying for that honoured role.

Barry (left) as a 'sixer' in Cub uniform with his elder brother.

Hagley had real shops, a sweet shop that was part of a terraced house and a toy shop. There was a toy tank on a transporter that I had set my heart on. It was bigger than a dinky toy, made of metal, with good detail and painted camouflage green. I wanted it. Seven shillings and sixpence the price tag said and that was many weeks of pocket money, plus birthday and Christmas money. After some considerable time (during which I was terrified they would sell this article to some undeserving boy) I managed to collect five shillings. I didn't want to wait any longer so went with mum to see what might be negotiated. Regretfully I was unable to purchase both the tank and the transporter, but came away with the tank. Nice ... but who, I wonder, bought the empty transporter?

We had an active Cub and Scout life, boys only. Girls had Guides and Brownies. We did 'Bob a Job Week', slaving for hours over vast driveways of weeds, only to be given a 'bob'. In contrast a kindly lady gave us a pair of shoes to clean, again for a 'bob'. My first experience of the capricious nature of labour and reward! I remember as I approached my teens, on one job, being shown how to weed a garden by this 'older' woman – and being utterly transfixed by her large breasts. I couldn't quite work out the feelings they engendered, except they felt good (the feelings) and held the promise of something more, though I didn't really know what that might be. Looking back I guess the 'older' woman was in her thirties. It seems, looking back and comparing my experience with today's culture, that my childhood had a certain innocence, a slow and steady growth from childhood to adulthood.

We loved games that involved imaginary battles, sticks for guns or swords, with a large garden or the woods to work out the various war scenarios. We even took a captive, Julian Jenkins, from down the road. He was an occasional friend and as we had read about tying up captives my brothers and I tied him to a tree at the bottom of the garden. We cogitated our next move, not sure about what to do next. Unfortunately at that moment mum shouted, 'Tea's ready!' and we impulsively ran to the house to see what joys awaited us. Unfortunately we forgot about our captive until some time later a worried mother knocked on the door asking if we had seen her son!

My brothers seemed to have a fascination with fire, maybe it was from my dad, who always seemed to have a bonfire on the go. I was eight when my five-year-old brother proudly put on his furry cowboy trousers and went down the garden. Upon poking the bonfire with a stick a spark flew onto his trousers and set them alight, he ran up the garden on fire, and a neighbour (who happened to be on a ladder and could see into the garden) shouted and called for help. I was nearby and pulled my brother to the ground, rolling him to extinguish the flames, thereby saving him from severe injury. I was promised a medal from the Scout Association, but did it ever materialise? No! Another lesson learnt about the fickle nature of adult promises.

Hagley Hall, a Palladian style manor house with its resident, Lord Cobham, sits above the village looking up to a beautiful park. In that park is a castle folly and a gamekeeper's cottage. I was lucky enough to stay in both, a friend's parents rented the cottage and my godfather rented the castle. No electricity at either, so oil lamps and, later, a generator provided lighting. But what a privilege to stay in such beautiful parkland, with few walkers. What a playground for two young boys! Also, behind our house were rolling fields and 'the Bog'. This was a swampy, marshy area where we used to play. You could poke a stick into the swamp, release the methane and ignite it with a match. We'd disappear with our sticks (air rifles later on) and roam the woods, the

The Austin brothers on holiday admiring an eel. Barry is second from right.

fields and lakes. By the time I was ten I could name most birds from their song, their eggs or flight patterns. We'd find nests and later visit to see the eggs, then the fledglings.

Books and comics seemed, even in the 1950s to be full of cowboys and indians and war stories with wicked 'Hun' soldiers fighting brave Tommies crying 'Achtung Himmel' or something similar. I used to make Airfix planes, Second World War planes such as Focke-Wulf or Spitfires. I'd sneak out onto the flat roof outside my bedroom and set fire to one wing, watching attentively as the flames and black smoke slowly consumed the plane, and pilot 'trapped' inside his cockpit. Rupert Bear annuals where Rupert flew to 'Coon Island' and we innocently read the stories and went to play with a black friend without linking the two. Friends had homes. We did not seem aware if they were big or small, whether parents were wealthy or poor. We knew no distinction. It was an age of innocence, a time when we were able to grow into adulthood at a measured pace, or so it seems looking back. At the time there must have been angst, anxiety, regret and fear, but I don't remember it.

After attending King Charles Grammar School, Kidderminster, Barry Austin took a year out to decide which career to follow. A memorable Christmas party at a firm of surveyors convinced him that this was the way forward. He became engaged to Debbie in his final year at college. After their marriage they settled in Cornwall, where Barry was employed by the county council. Their home overlooked the sea, which figured large in their activities. Barry and Debbie are committed Christians and their faith has also shaped their lives. They now live in Malvern where Barry is developing social enterprise organisations.

'My childhood was a warm time, punctuated with moments of revelation about the wider world at large. Are these rose-tinted perspectives? Probably, but then, those are the best ones aren't they?'

LUCY CONRAD

Lucy Conrad was born in North London in October 1967.

It was during the long, hot summer of 1976, when I was eight years old, that we all piled into our yellow Renault Twelve saloon car to make the journey from Oxford to Cornwall. We were so excited to be moving there, having visited the previous summer. Life was going to be one long holiday! My baby brother fitted snugly into an empty Fyffes banana box at my feet, while myself and younger brother and sister were strapped firmly into our blue seatbelts on the back seat. Rear seatbelts weren't compulsory at the time, but dad was very safety conscious, and once strapped in, we could barely move! There were no car radios then, so we had to make our own entertainment, which usually consisted of playing I-spy, along with the odd argument.

Another memorable journey was at the age of five. Dad and I travelled to Switzerland to visit my godmother on a combination of trains and a ferry, culminating in a sleeper train across France, we both had bottom bunks in a cabin of six, and ate Cadbury's Picnic bars throughout the night, a real treat!

It was in Switzerland that I first heard my dad speaking Polish, his mother tongue. My godmother's family were also Polish, and I remember sitting silently listening to them all, missing my mum and siblings, and eating very strange food. They were vegetarians, a rarity in England at the time, and I craved familiar food. I visited Lake Lucerne, saw snow for the first time and was chased by what I thought was a huge bear, but was actually a St Bernard dog trying to play with me. I've been slightly scared of dogs ever since.

I remember another dog, Prince, a boxer, who belonged to family friends in Birmingham where we lived for a few years in the early seventies. Prince had a distinctive and unforgettable 'doggy' smell. We visited often, the daughters were a little older than my sister and I, and I remember thinking how beautiful the mother was. She was Persian, exotic and glamorous, and used to make jewellery, her numerous ornate bracelets jangling tunefully on her arms as she moved. We ate pistachio nuts and collected hand-me-down dresses from the daughters, then would travel home at night via the brightly lit 'spaghetti junction'.

My earliest memories are from when we lived in Birmingham. I was born in London, and moved to Birmingham when I was two for a few years. We lived in a hospital house at first as dad worked as a doctor in the local hospital. I remember frequently visiting an Indian lady whose husband was also a doctor in one of the neighbouring houses, we couldn't communicate as she didn't speak English, but I think she was homesick and liked having some company, and I liked the ice lollies she gave me! While we lived there I remember my sister and I were confined to bed with mumps, and read comics all day in bed while recuperating, it felt like a treat not to have to go to school. It was also in Birmingham where we watched the Royal wedding of Princess Anne in 1973 at a neighbour's house, and I remember it was one of the first programmes I watched on a colour television. We still had a Phillips black and white television at the time in white plastic casing which looked quite futuristic. We weren't allowed to watch too much television, but l fondly remember children's television at the time, especially *The Clangers,* and we would all watch *Opportunity Knocks* on a Sunday night in our Ladybird dressing gowns before going to bed with Farley's rusks and hot milk.

We moved to Reading in 1974. I remember my sister and I 'digging' for treasure in a bit of scrubland near the house. We both managed to cut ourselves and were carted off to the local GP surgery for tetanus inoculations, and were both quite hysterical! I also remember my sister and I locking my brother, who was a toddler at the time in his bedroom, requiring a call to the fire brigade to get him out through the window. I enjoyed school, but my main recollection of primary school in Reading, was having to drink the small bottles of warm creamy milk we were given daily, which I hated, and I haven't liked the taste of milk ever since.

I was seven when we moved to Oxford. We lived in a modern house in a cul-de-sac, with a dreadful, but fashionable 'shag-pile' carpet in the sitting room chosen by the previous owners. We had equally nasty orange and brown bold, patterned wall paper in our bedroom, and bunk beds, where I remember listening to Queen's 'Bohemian Rhapsody' with a school friend every evening for weeks. Our primary school had a freezing outdoor swimming pool, where we learned to swim, and I had a very strict teacher, who mainly taught us italic handwriting. My sister and I started going to Brownies in Oxford, which I think we both preferred to school. My uncle, dad's younger brother, used to visit us from Poland every couple of years in the school holidays. He was more like an older brother, and never told us when he would arrive, but would appear sometime over the summer holidays, much to our excitement. In Oxford he tied all our bikes together one behind the other and we cycled around in circles until his flares got stuck in the chain and we all fell over like dominoes.

Lucy (left) with her sister Sonja (circa 1975).

When we finally settled in Cornwall, initially we lived a hospital flat while waiting to move into our new house. As mum couldn't drive we all walked every day to and from primary school near our new house about two miles away, eating marmite and cress sandwiches to keep us going on the way home. When we did finally move, we were all allowed pets. My sister and I chose guinea pigs from the local pet shop, and one of dad's colleagues provided rabbits for my brothers, one of whom was named Trouserleg by my youngest brother as he was the same colour as dad's trousers, and mum wouldn't let him name him Batman. The neighbours got used to mum waving lettuce leaves around the garden, and calling out 'trousers' for short! As a teenager Trouserleg and my younger brother weren't in my best books when I found the rabbit had chewed through the cables of my beloved record player, so I could no longer play my Prince records too loudly when in a teenage strop. 'Trousers' had preferred the peace of my pre-teenage years when I quietly read Enid Blyton books.

Being the eldest, I think I was always sent to try out new things. I learned to sail when I was nine along with two boys who were neighbours and a couple of years older than me. We had our lessons in a Wayfarer every day during summer half-term. It was cold and windy, and at the time I hated it, probably because I would rather have had the company of girls, but later on I was grateful I did it, as I now love sailing. I also went on a couple of summer adventure camps in Devon and Wales with a friend when we were eleven or twelve. They were quite tough: potholing, canoeing, trekking across Dartmoor carrying our tents for the night amongst other things, but also quite character building, and as a consequence, apart from potholing, I love outdoor pursuits.

While living in Cornwall, we often went to Brittany for summer holidays on the ferry from Plymouth. After a year of learning French at secondary school, I was volunteered to spend a week with a French family, as the son was a similar age to me. I spoke hardly any French, had nothing in common with him, and felt very hard done by. But, a few years later, I did an exchange with a girl in Paris, and loved it. She also enjoyed coming to Cornwall, and was pleasantly surprised when we didn't eat fish and chips out of newspaper every night as she had been led to believe the English do!

As we grew older and more independent we wanted to go out at weekends and during school holidays with our friends, so until we could all drive, we would get the train to Falmouth or St Ives and spend the day on the beach, or shopping in Plymouth. Our parents took it in turns to take us to the local village discos in church halls. We dressed in our regulation eighties clothes, frilly shirts, knickerbockers and ankle boots, and far too much make-up. At one time, I was reprimanded by the deputy head of my comprehensive school for wearing too much make up, obviously not a fan of lilac eye shadow and lipstick!

We used to visit my grandparents a lot in Sussex as children, and eventually they moved to Cornwall to be nearer to us. I remember once telling gran that I wanted to be a dentist when I was older. She couldn't understand and wondered why I wanted to do it as it was a 'man's job'. She was born in 1898, and was very traditional, thinking it was wrong for women to work as they took jobs from the men. I think it made me more determined to show what I was capable of!

My Polish grandmother visited a few times from Poland, but could hardly speak any English. Poland was still a Communist country when I was a child, and dad didn't return for many years after he emigrated until the fall of communism. Babcia (Polish for grandma) was a good cook, and made lovely Polish apple cakes and traditional Christmas poppy seed cake for us. I still try to make it, but it's never as good.

Lucy achieves her ambition to become a dentist.
Birmingham University Graduation Day (1991).

Lucy Conrad realised her ambition to go to university to study dentistry, and qualified from Birmingham in 1991. She returned to work in Cornwall, where she loved living by the sea, and took up sailing again. After a few years the bright lights of London beckoned, and she enjoyed all it had to offer before moving to the Cotswolds, slowly edging her way back to her beloved Cornwall. She has worked full-time as a dentist for twenty years, but has always pursued other interests from tango-dancing to jewellery making. She loves travelling and outdoor pursuits, and has recently enjoyed a couple of trips trekking and camping in the wilds of Patagonia, Argentina.

'I have wonderful childhood memories, and loved growing up in a big family and experiencing different places and people. It is interesting how different my childhood and my aspirations were from those of my grandparents, and how different it will be again for future generations.'

REBECCA EDWARDS
Rebecca Edwards was born in Truro, Cornwall, in March 1973

The sun shone consistently throughout the 1970s. The only time that the weather changed was when snow fell in abundance on a couple of occasions and I spent hours of fun outside our large garden trying to convince a kitchen tray to become a sledge. Similarly, rain fell once when I was being picked up from Beacon Infants School and informed that I had a treat waiting for me at home from Godfather Guy. It was a French surprise so it had even more value than anything local: a doll dressed from head to toe in orange.

There was a certain smell and feel about the air which appeared sometime in June. It was the smell of the summer holidays. This period started with permission to go out into the garden bare-footed and the pleasure of being able to feel grass between your toes, sit on the home-made swing hung amongst the fruit trees beside the solid garden wall and look at the smiles on the faces of the daisies and dandelions. I lived for the summer holidays which included our regular trips to Devon or Yorkshire for family walking holidays. I wasn't to travel abroad until I was fourteen with a trip to Brittany and that was a huge anti climax. I saw it as a carbon copy of Cornwall with the inconvenience of a different language and encumbrance of my own family. Little was I to know at that stage that in later life I would be living and working in France for three years.

I had the luxury of being born and brought up in a large farmhouse in Cornwall, with three sisters as close companions, where the surrounding garden was our entire universe. Here paper lollipops were

Study of Rebecca with her mother, Veronica, and oranges (1976).

exchanged for hogwort seed and Wonder Woman and rounders were tirelessly played when the climbing frame was being given a break and the bike had already had a few sessions around the garden following along the trails cut by the lawn mower. There are occasional memories of visitors joining in these games; Lexa the size seven feet primary school child who told us about UFOs which ensured that we always went into the house on time during summer evenings so that we would be safe before their appearance in the sky. However, by and large pure bliss was when we were visitor-less and able to romp unashamedly around the garden. Cousins were the exception to the rule and their two-week cricket-filled stay with regular trips to the beach, all in bright sunshine, provided an even greater sense of contentment.

On the whole, I didn't like school. Anna and I were one rather than twins, starting school at the age of four and a half where the order of the day was sandpit, plastic bricks and the Wendy House. We adored Mrs Lloyd and responded to her firm but fair approach and warmth. Snacks for break time were blue-tacked to the piano. We longed to have disco crisps to attach to the furniture but alas we had the ongoing disappointment of an apple or a piece of cheese. On occasion we had school lunches and I have a lasting memory of greasy crisps. That was perhaps the start of the generation of fussy eaters. Claire Downing would only eat Kit Kats.

After Mrs Lloyd it was downhill all the way with a progression from light-hearted to more persistent playground bullying. Not enough to bring about immediate school action but enough to impact on the increasing negative influence of hormones. However, this began during the later days of primary school and at secondary school. Bassett Junior School will be fondly remembered for an introduction to music with Miss Martin leading the Camborne inter-school singing competition and bringing about a performance of *Joseph* and *Aladdin*. It also influenced my thinking on education at an early age as I witnessed at first hand bright children slipping gradually behind in class due to their social background. Zena Murton was a gifted athlete and mathematician, but at the age of eight was being sent out to sell bingo tickets on behalf of her father. I shall never forget witnessing traveller children being whisked off to have a shower and scrubbed up only to return dirty to school the next day and wondering whether or not the school had done the right thing. In those days there appeared to be substantial support for children with special educational needs in the form of a special unit. There seemed to be numerous hearing tests, sight tests, weight tests, Nitty Nora the flea explorer and of course free milk before it was whisked away by Margaret Thatcher.

I do not recall the 1970s being a great decade for food connoisseurs. Living in the rural South West we had the luxury of mussels collected from local beaches and occasional crab legs. However, English cuisine in those parts had not been influenced widely by other cultures so shepherds' pie, stuffed marrow, broccoli cheese, dumplings and stew were the menu of the day. Unlike other countries there wasn't the same culture of going out to eat as a family unless Paddy the honorary family member came to stay. To walk all the way from Lamorna to Mousehole and to be fed ploughman's lunch was often a bitter disappointment. Better to be given a pasty and a glass of lemonade. Fortunately, my parents had lived in France for a brief spell so the table was regularly blessed with a bottle of red wine and we would be permitted at a very early age to have a small glass with our meal. Needless to say that this did not lead to alcoholism but I believe instead steered us away from the path of binge drinking. We were brought up to eat everything on our plates because of the starving children in the world. On occasion I thought that the starving children in the world were more than welcome to my bread pudding and I'd have given away Ida William's cake and its sour cream topping with great pleasure.

Television played an important role in the 1970s. We would sometimes be dropped off at home by a parent whose daughters attended the same school and watched television until our parents returned home. Someone would be on guard and then we'd swoop to ensure that it was switched off on time. I was recently informed of someone who did similarly within her family. Her parents would come home and feel the television set for its warmth so on one occasion they decided to pour water all over it to cool it down before their parents could feel it.

There was a great deal of brilliant trash on television including the *Dukes of Hazzard*, *Wonder Woman* and *Chips*. We loved the *Muppet Show* and I remember being devastated when I missed an episode, having to be whisked off to a family friend, who was a GP, after too creatively imagining that the family cat was a tiger and running away from it only to find myself falling headfirst into the dining room dresser and biting through my tongue. Now let's not forget the legacy of Oliver Postgate: *Bagpuss* and *Ivor the Engine,* programmes which very much epitomise the innocence and creativity of that time.

As for music, this was the decade of Abba. Abba dominated the music scene. You could even purchase a Sindy record player that with the right batteries would play Waterloo. Whilst Queen and Fleetwood Mac were around at the time, we were only able to discover them as a family during the late 1980s. Instead, we followed a different course and carried on the tradition of listening to The Beatles and the Seekers whilst also being provided with a taste of world music in the form of Mariam Makeba and 'Ochee Ca Ca Oh' by who knows?

Sunday Mass played an important role within the family weekly calendar. I never minded going but was glad to leave the mantilla-wearing crowd of Camborne Church to the more brightly coloured brigade in Truro. We weren't the slightest bit interested in the good looking altar boys … and so went to additional services for holy days of obligation with great enthusiasm. I didn't mind going to catechism either with the smiling, gentle nun Sister Jemma. I would draw endless pictures of Mary and Saints into my blue exercise book and this was an opportunity to receive easy praise for nominal effort.

I was fortunate to have dedicated parents who saw education as an integral part of our up-bringing, even if that meant picture competitions after a day off school to go to Stithians Show. In hindsight we were quite spoilt with a beautiful home, copious quantities of books, paper and pens and toys not to mention family security. I look back with increasing gratitude that we were not shipped off to child minders or holiday clubs during the school holidays. We were not fashionable or so we thought. However, how many children now wear nylon flares and parkas? The exploitation of children through advertising was beginning to creep into childhood with the growth of the influence of television. Divorce was not as evident as it is today and I remember when a classmate informed me that her parents were separating. Perhaps this was just my naivety coming from a sheltered, stable home background.

To quote Mary Hopkins, another influential figure in our 1970s 'those were the days my friends'. However, I recall the shadow that hung over us in 1979 when Margaret Thatcher won the election and I felt this Conservative cloud hang over me until the very end of the 1980s with the start of my four-year stint at Leeds University.

Rebecca prides herself on never having voted Conservative subsequent to what felt like the oppressive years of Tory government. She went on to study Politics and Spanish at the University of Leeds. However, the idea of a year abroad in South America enticed her to complete her studies in Spanish and Portuguese. She initially started her working life in further, secondary and higher education and experienced teaching at a sinking school in South London as well as a two-year stint at the University of the Sorbonne in Paris. Whilst Rebecca does not have children of her own she is very proud of her nieces and nephews and indeed currently works for a national children's charity. Her interests have been strongly influenced by a childhood spent predominantly outdoors and by stories of her parents' travels in Swaziland and France. Rebecca is a keen amateur tennis player, canoeist and rambler who plays world music on the guitar.

TIMELINE OF BRITISH SOCIAL HISTORY: 1976–1999

1976

Harold Wilson resigned as Prime Minister, succeeded by James Callaghan.

A prolonged heat wave in June and July led to the worst drought in UK since 1720s. The peak temperature of 35·9°C, recorded in Cheltenham.

Average rate of inflation was 16·5%.

The number of deaths (681,000) exceeded the number of births (676,000), the only year in which this happened during the century.

Cod War between Britain and Iceland.

James Hunt became Formula One World Champion.

A 20 year study by Doll and Peto of the smoking habits of 35,000 doctors concluded that ⅓ died from the habit.

Jeffrey Archer published his first novel *Not a Penny More, Not a Penny Less*.

Queen released 'Bohemian Rhapsody': the third most popular British pop song of all time.

The Queen sent an e-mail.

1977

Government admitted that inflation had pushed up prices by 70% in three years.

Geoffrey Boycott scored the hundredth century of his career against Australia at Headingley.

Foreign cars outsold British-built cars for the first time.

Firefighters went on strike for the first time and were replaced by the army manning 'Green Goddesses'.

Abba released 'Knowing Me, Knowing You' which became a number one hit in the charts.

Release of the film *Saturday Night Fever* starring John Travolta.

1978

End of the Lib-Lab pact resulted in a minority Labour Government.

Inflation fell to 9·9%.

Ian Botham became the first cricketer to score a century and take eight wickets in a Test Match.

Motability, a charity providing cars for disabled people, founded.

First broadcast of *The Hitchhiker's Guide to the Galaxy,* devised as a radio series by Douglas Adams.

1979

'The Winter of Discontent' with 10,000s of public sector workers on strike.

James Callaghan lost a vote of confidence in the House of Commons.

General Election won by the Conservatives with Margaret Thatcher becoming the first female Prime Minister in UK (May).

First elections to the European Parliament with turnout of 32%.

Assassination of Conservative MP Airey Neave (by INLA) and Lord Mountbatten (by Provisional IRA).

Waterpoint ambush in which 18 British soldiers were killed in Northern Ireland by an IRA bomb.

Largest number of days lost by strikes since 1926.

The first J D Wetherspoon pub opened in Haringey.

1980

Britain became self sufficient in oil.

The economy slid into recession and inflation rose to 21·8%.

Collapse of the Alexander Kielland North Sea accommodation platform with the loss of 123 lives.

Miners' leaders demanded a 37% pay increase.

Housing Act came into force giving tenants of three years standing the right to buy their homes.

In the face of mounting criticism of her economic policy Margaret Thatcher made her 'The Lady's not for turning' speech.

John Lennon's song '(Just Like) Starting Over' reached number one in the charts. One week later he was shot dead in New York.

1981

Population reached 56·3 million.

Prince Charles married Lady Diana Spencer at St Paul's Cathedral. The ceremony watched by a television audience of 30 million.

The Social Democratic Party (SDP) formed by 'The Gang of Four'.

Peter Sutcliffe, aka the Yorkshire Ripper, found guilty of murdering 13 women in the Leeds area.

Unemployment rose above 2·6 million.

The first case of AIDS diagnosed in the UK.

Penlee lifeboat disaster. Both the lifeboat and the coaster *Union Star* were lost with all hands.

The telegram discontinued after 139 years.

First public demonstration of a CD in UK on BBC television in *Tomorrow's World*.

Queen's album 'Greatest Hits' was released: the best selling album in the UK of all time.

Michelle Magorian published *Goodnight Mr Tom*.

1982

Start of the Falklands War with a Royal Navy task force leaving Portsmouth bound for the South Atlantic (April).

The nuclear submarine HMS *Conqueror* sank the Argentine cruiser General Belgrano (May).

Argentine troops on the Falkland Islands surrendered (July), The casualties of military personnel were 255 British and 649 Argentines. Three civilians were also killed.

Roy Jenkins won the Hillhead by-election for the SDP.

Unemployment reached three million (13·8% of work force).

The first album produced as a CD: Billy Joel's *52nd Street*.

Sue Townsend published *The Secret Diary of Adrian Mole, Aged 13¾*.

1983

- The Conservative Party with Margaret Thatcher as PM won a landslide election victory with a majority of 144 seats.
- Neil Kinnock replaced Michael Foot as leader of the Labour Party.
- CD discs and players on sale in the UK.
- The one pound coin was introduced.
- Licence granted to Cellnet and Vodafone to provide a national cellular network.
- Compulsory use of seat belts by car drivers introduced.
- Brinks-MAT robbery in London. 6,800 gold bars worth £26 million were stolen.

1984

- Brighton hotel bombing in which the Provisional IRA attempted to assassinate the High Command of the Conservative Party. Five people killed including MP Anthony Berry. Margaret Thatcher was unhurt.
- The miners strike began in March.
- The iconic Morris and Triumph car brands were discontinued. The Japanese firm Nissan signed a deal to make cars in Britain and chose a site near Sunderland.
- Unemployment reached 3·26 million.
- The pound note was withdrawn after being in circulation for 150 years.
- Cinema audiences fell to 501 million.
- *Thomas the Tank Engine* series began on television.
- Band Aid's charity song 'Do They Know Its Christmas?' was number one in the charts over the Christmas period.

1985

- 56 people killed in a fire at the Valley Parade stadium in Bradford during a football match.
- 55 people killed in an air disaster at Manchester airport.
- Manufacture of Peugeot 309 began at Ryton, Coventry, becoming the first 'foreign' car to be made in Britain.
- Dire Straits were the first to sell one million copies of an album on CD *(Brothers in Arms)*.
- Ernie Wise made the first mobile phone call in Britain.

Launch of the television soap *East Enders*.

1986
'Big Bang' at the London Stock Exchange which was computerised and opened to foreign companies.

UK and France announced plans to construct the Channel Tunnel.

Launch of the *Today* newspaper which pioneered the use of computer photo setting and full colour off-set printing.

First edition of the *Independent* newspaper.

GCSE examination replaced both GCE O-level and CSE exams for 14-year-olds.

Sir Alex Ferguson became manager of Manchester United, the start of an unprecedented reign in top-flight football.

1987
General election won by the Conservative Party (June). Margaret Thatcher secured her third term as PM.

The Church of England Synod voted to allow the ordination of women.

MS Herald of Free Enterprise capsized leaving Zeebrugge harbour with a loss of 193 lives.

8,016 diagnoses of HIV reported in UK.

British Rail established a world speed record for diesel traction of 148 miles per hour (238.9 kilometres per hour) with an InterCity 125 between Darlington and York.

Construction started on the Channel Tunnel.

Corporal punishment in state schools banned by Parliament.

Golliwogs banned from Enid Blyton books and replaced by gnomes.

1988
SDP merged with the Liberal Party to form the Social and Liberal Democratic Party under the leadership of Paddy Ashdown. Now known as the Lib Dems.

Elizabeth Butler-Sloss became the first woman to be appointed Lord Justice of Appeal.

Most provisions of the Education Reform Act came into effect, including introduction of National Curriculum with key stages.

Piper Alpha oil rig exploded in North Sea with 167 workers killed.

Lockerbie disaster. Bomb exploded on Pan Am flight 103 with 270 people killed.

Kylie Minogue reached number one in the charts with 'I Should Be So Lucky'.

Rain Man (directed by Barry Levinson, starring Dustin Hoffman and Tom Cruise) was one of the most popular films.

1989

Margaret Thatcher, George Bush and Mikhail Gorbachov declared the end of the Cold War.

UNCRC ratified by the UN General Assembly.

Hillsborough disaster. 95 fans were killed in a crush during the FA cup semi-final match between Nottingham Forest and Liverpool.

Keyworth air disaster. 44 people were killed when a British Midlands Boeing 737 crashed on the M1 near East Midlands Airport.

Sky Television started broadcasting the first satellite television service in Britain.

Television premiere of the animated film *A Grand Day Out with Wallace and Gromit*.

1990

Margaret Thatcher resigned after failing to win an outright victory in the contest for leadership of the Conservative Party (November); succeeded by John Major.

200,000 protested against the proposed Poll Tax in London.

15,166 diagnoses of HIV reported in UK.

Hurricane force winds killed 39 people in January whilst 14 people were killed by storms in February.

Scare about BSE affecting humans. Agriculture Minister John Gummer fed a hamburger to his five-year-old daughter to allay the Nation's fears.

Tim Berners-Lee and Robert Cailliau proposed a 'hypertext system', starting the modern internet.

1991
Population reached 57·8 million. 31% of population over the age of 50.
The Gulf War began.
UK finally agreed that every child has all the rights listed in UNCRC.
Tim Bernes-Lee established the first web site at CERN.
The computer retailer PC World opened its first store in Croydon.
The final phase of the M40 was opened through Oxfordshire.
27 people died as a result of gale force winds.
Roald Dahl replaced Enid Blyton as the most popular author of children's books.
Bryan Adams' song '(Everything I Do) I Do It For You' dominated the charts.

1992
General Election won by Conservatives under John Major. *The Sun* newspaper claimed the credit.
Neil Kinnock resigned as leader of Labour Party. He had been the longest-serving leader of the Opposition. Replaced by John Smith.
Government suspended membership of the Exchange Rate Mechanism (Black Wednesday).
Three women rose to prominence in public life: Betty Boothroyd as Speaker of the House of Commons, Stella Rimmington as Director of MI5 and Barbara Mills as Director of Public Prosecutions.
Unemployment rate was 9·4%.
Ethnic minorities accounted for 5% of the British population.
Most retailers withdrew vinyl records from stock.

1993
UK Independence Party formed.
VAT added to domestic fuel bills by Chancellor Norman Lamont.
The Child Support Agency formed.
Railways Act passed by John Major's government which led to the privatisation of British Rail.
A high-speed train made the first journey from France to England through the Channel Tunnel.
Rate of inflation 1·3%.

OPCS survey showed that 23% of 15-year-olds were regular smokers.

Sebastian Faulkes published *Birdsong*.

Terry Deary published *The Terrible Tudors*, the first in the 'Horrible History' series.

1994

John Smith, leader of the Labour Party died suddenly; succeeded by Tony Blair.

First meeting between British government and Sinn Fein for 70 years took place.

Channel Tunnel opened by the Queen and President Francois Mitterand.

Privatisation of the coal industry: 20,000 miners employed.

The first digital cameras produced for the domestic market.

The first National Lottery draw took place.

Louis de Bernieres published *Captain Corelli's Mandolin*.

'Love Is All Around' sung by Wet Wet Wet, dominated the charts.

1995

Barings Bank, Britain's oldest merchant bank, collapsed following losses of 1.4 billion dollars made by rogue trader Nick Leeson.

War in Bosnia and Herzegovina. British forces sent to Sarajevo.

Internet based on dial-up systems where the speed (typically 38 kilobytes per second) was limited by bandwidths.

Frank Bruno won the WBC heavyweight championship.

Karl Jenkins released his album *Adiemus: Songs of Sanctuary*.

1996

The Conservative government majority gradually declined to 0.

First passenger train companies started operating following privatisation of British Rail.

First genetically modified food went on sale.

Dolly the sheep, the first mammal to be cloned from an adult cell, was born at Roslin Institute, Scotland.

Government announced plans to make handguns illegal following the Dunblane massacre in which 16 children and their teacher were killed.

29% of men and 28% of women were smokers (a small rise on 1970).

1997

Labour Party won a landslide victory with a majority of 179, which ended 18 years in opposition. Tony Blair became PM.

Death of Princess Diana and Dodi Fayed in an accident in the Pont de l'Alma road tunnel in Paris. Three million mourners and onlookers attended her funeral in London.

Average size of completed family fell to 1·7 children.

Infant mortality 5·8 deaths per 1,000 births.

The number of vehicles registered was 26·9 million. Road fatalities: 3,599.

Mobile phone ownership reached 20%.

J K Rowling published the first of the 'Harry Potter' series with *Harry Potter and the Philosopher's Stone*.

Teletubbies introduced to children's television.

1998

The Good Friday agreement signed by the British and Irish governments and main political parties in Northern Ireland.

29 people killed by a car bomb in Omagh: the worst terrorist atrocity in the history of the troubles in Northern Ireland.

The Human Rights Act passed.

Miners employed in the coal industry fell to 9,000.

Home ownership of computers rose to 29%.

1999

The purchasing power of the pound fell from £1 in 1900 to the equivalent of 1·5p.

Life expectancy for boys: 75 years; and 80 years for girls.

Owner-occupation of houses rose to 68%.

Introduction of the first mobile phones able to send e-mails and use the net.

Corporal punishment banned in private schools.

Government announced plans to introduce a ban on tobacco advertising.

Karl Jenkins composed *The Armed Man: A Mass for Peace*. The music had been commissioned by the Royal Armouries to mark the millennium.

PETER COUSINS
Peter Cousins was born in Truro, Cornwall, in December 1981

I grew up not only in the dying years of the twentieth century, but in the final decades of the second millennium, turning eighteen just before the year 2000. It would be tempting to analyse such a childhood in a highly contextualised fashion. How it was to grow up in an impoverished part of the country during the Thatcher years, as the final tin mines spluttered their way towards closure and how the turn of the century offered at least the prospect of fresh optimism, epitomised in the construction just up the road of the forward-looking Eden Project. I have nevertheless tried to avoid casting too much hindsight over these reflections, instead drilling back down into my memories of activities, thoughts and impressions as I experienced them at the time.

I have two clear memories from my first five years, although I am no longer sure which came first. On one occasion, my mum was in hospital about to give birth to my younger sister. My grandma and aunty had come to help out. As with many young children, I loved trains and I would watch them come and go from my bedroom window. Grandma told me that they would take my brother and I to Falmouth on the branch line that day. A picnic was prepared and we found a table on the train. Such was the attraction of the ride itself, we did not alight in Falmouth, but came straight home on the return trip!

The second memory stems from the time my dad took me into our street to try out a bicycle belonging to a neighbour. After satisfactorily arranging the stabilisers, dad gave me a push and off I went. Our road is a cul-de-sac on a downhill gradient. The bike gathered momentum and, owing to the fact that the brakes had not been properly secured, I had no means of stopping it. I wound up in a neighbour's garage at the bottom of the street and emerged, crying, to find my dad and our neighbour in fits of laughter, which to my young mind seemed an even greater injustice than having been placed on a dysfunctional vehicle.

These stories reveal two elements of my early years, that we were a close family, and that life on our street was convivial. Mum's family lived in Plymouth, and there was frequent transit in both directions across the Tamar, so that my grandma, my aunties, uncles and cousins were never far removed from our upbringing. Dad's family lived further away, but they were not out of the loop altogether. Our grandmas spoiled us (pancakes and KFC were real treats) and we would never fail to get excited when we were all due to meet up.

Our neighbours were our fondest friends. We were particularly close to two other families, and between us there would come to be ten children, plus those of other households on the street. We were generally at liberty to play in the cul-de-sac, or in any of our houses. We all had bikes (most of the time they worked!) and we would play hide-and-seek for hours. Unusually for Truro, the two closest families were of South African and Mauritian origin, and although I was aware of some differences (yellow rice and samosas featured commonly in shared food), they seemed much less important than the serious business of enjoying oneself.

Going to school altered nothing of these formative realities, although it did bring changes. New faces came into the picture; the boy I sat next to on my first day at primary school, Ben, became my best friend. There were also books to read, times-tables to learn and PE to participate in. While at primary school I enjoyed taking part in sport but I soon realised that my place was on the sidelines: in particular those of Home Park, where Plymouth Argyle toiled away. My interest in football was awakened by England's campaign in Italia '90, where they came oh-so-close to the final, and where Gazza cried. The following season my uncle took me to my first Argyle match, which coincided suspiciously with a downturn in their fortunes.

Our holidays followed a pattern held dear within the family. Every summer we frequented the small village of Polzeath, with its grand beach and spectacular surroundings, usually with some of mum's relatives. We stayed in a caravan park about ten minutes walk from the beach, and the approach of the roving ice-cream van represented the highlight of each day; as we were on holiday, we were allowed one every day. Even as a child it was obvious that Cornwall at its best provided for the stuff of memories. Nevertheless, in an early sign that I would later catch the 'travel-bug' in an irreversible fashion, I began to wonder why we would not travel abroad. My first journey outside of Britain was, perhaps inevitably, not with my family but in my final year of primary school, on a French exchange to Niort. That trip must have broken the taboo, as family holidays from then onwards involved crossing the Channel.

As time went on and secondary education approached, I became aware that our family home fell in the catchment for Richard Lander School, while my primary school (St Mary's) tended to feed Penair. Throughout my primary school years, friendships from my street were probably still of more consequence than those I had at St Mary's. All the same, I was faced with the prospect of being parted from people with whom I had shared the previous seven years. It came as a relief to discover that my parents would apply for me to have a transfer across town, which was approved. Ben and I chose to go into the same form together at Penair. Moving to secondary school was exciting and daunting in equal measure, although from the perspective of year seven, those doing GCSEs appeared untouchable and it seemed unreal that I would ever reach that stage myself.

I worked hard at Penair. There was always pressure (sometimes unspoken, sometimes articulated) to disobey the rules, but I was never really capable of seriously rebelling against my teachers' instructions and consequently performed well, achieving good marks throughout the five years I was there. Nor was the pressure so strong that 'being keen', as it was known, caused any real isolation socially. On the contrary, at Penair the composition of our friendship group shifted away from home in favour of school friends. And even by those standards, our tutor group was exceptional: by year nine or ten, they were more or less one and the same, with a bit of ebb and flow. I remember one December the deputy head asked, flabbergasted, why the entirety of the form went late-night shopping together.

In some ways, however, I was not a 'typical' pupil. Perhaps due in part to my commitments to the piano and the double bass (the lessons for which I arranged around PE lessons), I did not enjoy much of the music which was popular then, something which raised eyebrows. Nor did I have a girlfriend while at school, which in itself did not particularly concern me, as I was fairly shy about that sort of thing, although some friends felt compelled to ask me about it. I also never really lapsed from going to church, which even then was something which people generally accepted as being a personal choice, if the topic came up at all.

Neither my family nor any of my friends were budding politicians, but I remember both general elections in

Peter Cousins, aged sixteen, dressed for the leaving ball at Truro College.

the nineties. In 1992 I recall our Mauritian neighbour came round for the results, and at one stage in the evening, the Conservatives were behind. I asked why, if Labour were ahead, there was a problem, and was confused by the foreboding nature of the answer, that the counts of the safe Tory seats hadn't come in yet. There were no such issues in 1997, when 'New' Labour swept to power and the relief was tangible, even in such places as Cornwall which reliably voted for the Lib Dems. By then I understood a little more about why the mood of the country had literally changed overnight.

During those final three years before the turn of the century, time began to speed up. I did four A-Levels at Truro College, where I fell for Spanish and consolidated my reputation as a linguist. Before I knew it, I found myself with an offer to study German and Spanish at Oxford, a prospect which I had laughed off not long before. We also installed the internet at home, having only purchased our first computer in 1992. I signed up for my first e-mail address (pistolpete@hotmail.com) on the basis of a nickname I had been given at Penair, and booked my first cheap flight online. The communications revolution was underway and, although temporarily threatened by the spectre of the Millennium Bug, added to the new found sense of dynamism.

The atmosphere cultivated at Truro College was comparable with that of university, and at that point my parents also decided it was time to let me make my own mistakes. Though I would have more growing up to do at Oxford, I could tell my childhood was coming to an end. I actually realise now that it was quite an idyllic upbringing. Not all of my peers could count on a loving, unified nuclear and extended family. And Truro, unlike many other parts of Cornwall, always appeared to weather the economic or social storms which crossed its path. If there were problems in the family or beyond, I was well-sheltered from them. I marvel now that, as children, we would be outdoors on the street or the beach as much as we were, given how much one hears today about the dangers that exist, or the attraction of video games and the like. I suspect that has as much to do with the nature of Cornwall itself as the era; and on our street now, things haven't changed that much. Youngsters can still be seen riding up and down the hill. Inevitably my appreciation for Cornwall has grown as I have moved on. Before I went up to Oxford, a friend's dad gave me a piece of advice: never forget where you are from and how it has shaped you. Perhaps this only becomes clear as the years go on.

Peter Cousins graduated from Oxford University with a BA in Spanish and German. Following graduation he worked with asylum-seekers in inner-city Glasgow, with homeless people in Cambridge and for local government in Cornwall. These experiences sowed the seeds of an increasing interest in peace work, and in 2007 Peter obtained an MA in Conflict Resolution from Bradford University. He then worked in Columbia for two years, combining his love of the Spanish-speaking world with his commitment to conflict and peace issues. Peter is currently working as a community mediator for a Bradford-based organisation.

CATHERINE PITT
Catherine Pitt was born in Norwich in March 1985

My earliest memory is going to visit my mum in Norfolk and Norwich hospital following her operation. I remember taking an old-fashioned lift to her ward with my dad. The lift had a steel grating instead of a door and I was afraid of falling out. Arriving at what seemed like the top floor of a skyscraper, I recall the flaking paint on every surface and the general shabbiness of the hospital. Mum's room seemed like a prison cell, the metal bedstead and the walls had the same flaking paint as the rest of the hospital. Someone had thoughtfully bought her a helium cat-shaped balloon to brighten up the room, and it was floating and bobbing up and down at the end of the bed like a beach ball in water. There was a sense that they had locked my mother away in this place and done terrible things to her against her will. I remember, by no means for the last time, thinking how brave and stoical she was in coping with adverse situations as they arose. She smiled at me and I wanted to take her home and away from this place. This aversion to hospitals was a feature of the era, they seemed monumentally terrifying in the 1980s and 1990s. This was before the days when hospitals became home to amenities such as WRVS coffee shops.

Thankfully one person who never seemed ill enough to be in hospital was Grandpa Pitt. The one time he went to hospital he epically walked home after a foot operation as though it was an everyday occurrence. He possessed an energetic spirit and loved long walks, much longer than I would have chosen myself. I remember thinking I wanted to be as active as him when I was eighty. He seemed to never go to bed, he was up long before I was and seemed to go to Mass every day. He never appeared to get tired or unhappy, remaining quick-witted and full of fun. I remember him leaving for Mass with a rose in his buttonhole (he always wore a jacket and tie) and on his return the rose had disappeared. On asking him about it, he jovially told me he had given it to a lady he didn't know at the church. I remember the excitement of going to visit him, looking forward to playing in his big garden where plum trees and gooseberry bushes grew. The bottom of the garden seemed very secluded, a tangle of vegetation in urban Harrow. Coming from rural Norfolk I appreciated being able to walk to the shops with grandpa, shops where everyone seemed to know him and talk to him like a friend and seemed to love him as much as we did. Unlikely as it seems now, Harrow was an exciting place as a child. Of particular interest to me was the thriving Asian community. I remember the aura of exoticism and mystery surrounding their clothes and spices. English food and clothing seemed pale and drab by comparison. Grandpa's neighbours were Indian and I was fascinated by their lives which seemed much more interesting than ours. I enjoyed listening to the singing and clapping coming from their house, which grandpa explained was in celebration of their daughter's place awarded at Oxford University. I was always sorry to leave and return to the less cosmopolitan Norfolk.

Another place I was always sorry to leave was Cornwall, where we used to visit Aunty Veronica and Uncle Richard and my cousins. The beaches seemed a world away from those I was familiar with in Norfolk. Rock pools in particular are unheard of in Norfolk. Cornwall remains sunny in my memory, rainy days are all but eclipsed. On one occasion we broke the journey in Devon, staying at a farmhouse bed and breakfast in Morton

School holiday fun at home in Alpington near Norwich (circa 1993). Catherine aged eight pretending to be a cowgirl on a mute horse with a placid temperament.

Hampstead. I remember thinking that this was a truer reflection of the English countryside than Norfolk was. Devon and Cornwall felt very remote and beautiful, I managed to catch a tick from one of the fields of sheep by way of example. Later, I would visit Cornwall without my parents and the place never lost its appeal as a place of maritime beauty.

I will always remember the times when I was allowed to go to places without my parents. Living in the countryside, most places were only accessible by car. This meant that being allowed into Norwich by myself on the bus was a big deal at the age of thirteen. I caught the bus with my school friends, which took about fifty minutes (a journey that took about fifteen minutes by car). As a teenager in the 1990s it was expected that you would loiter in a major city with your friends, apparently doing very little. Before the trip my mum requested a list of all the places we were planning to go to as she was anxious at the thought of us wandering around Norwich aimlessly. Needless to say we rather did wander around aimlessly as none of us had any source of income. I remember thinking how exciting it was to not have to rely on anyone else, a sentiment that has never left me. Obviously I was not allowed to go on holiday alone in my early teenage years. I went abroad for the first time to Calais with a school trip and wondered if the air and scenery would be much different from England. We went on a coach and took Le Shuttle across to Calais. The inside of the Le Shuttle resembled a nuclear bunker, devoid of any kind of amenities. When we arrived we saw Calais town hall, went to a French supermarket and then took the Shuttle back again. Essentially it seemed very much like England and a lot of effort to make the crossing just for a single afternoon. The vast majority of my school friends on the trip had already been on holiday abroad numerous times so they were equally unimpressed. In the 1990s it began to be expected that families would take holidays abroad rather than staying in the UK. Foreign travel had become cheaper and more convenient, facilitated by newer modes of transport such as the shuttle.

Other technological advances impacted on my early teenage years. I recall my first attempt to use the internet and being dumbfounded by it. Dad had a dial-up internet connection on a computer that he had inherited from my cousin Anna. Most of my school friends had started using the internet and were beginning to use 'chat rooms' to talk to each other in the evenings. They explained how they had been responsible for incurring astronomic phone bills as a result of their chat-room use. I don't remember feeling any desire to join them, preferring to see them face-to-face or talk over the phone. The internet seemed an expensive and precious resource whose use was rationed. Accessing information was painstakingly slow and I remember thinking either the internet was overrated or I lacked patience. I remember first sending an e-mail to a friend but finding that the recipient had not known about the e-mail until I saw them face to face and told them about it. At the time this seemed to defeat the purpose, as this was in the days before it was normal practice to check e-mails regularly.

Another feature of my early teenage years was the emergence of boy bands, who seemed to be clean-living characters who lived safe and uneventful lives. Their success seemed to focus on their personal lifestyles and good looks rather than their music. It was expected that you would not only have listened to their music, but have their posters on your wall, and have stickers with their faces on virtually everything you owned. I forget the names of my preferred bands of the era. They all blend into one in my memory like their generic characters. It wasn't until a year or so later that I tired of these boy bands, heavily influenced by what my older brothers and sister were listening to. My brothers and sister seemed to have very developed and sophisticated taste in music which appealed to me. This began to develop my passion for music, and the realisation that it is a potent essence and language of human emotion. I started to learn the trumpet, having lessons at our old house further up the street, and the instrument quickly became an essential means of self-expression for feelings it was difficult to verbalise.

As a teenager it is often difficult to express oneself though the usual channels, and to make sense of events seen in the news. I was twelve at the time of Princess Diana's death and we watched the media coverage on television. I saw the public outpouring of hysterical grief, a feeling that was infectious. I felt that it was almost the end of an era in a sense, and it also came at a time of some big changes in my life. I was unduly unsettled by this event as I was at an age when I wanted everything to stay the same. We had recently moved house, it was not long since Grandpa Pitt and Granny Donoghue had died and I had just started at secondary school. It also seemed to be an excuse for the general public to air their own personal grief from life events. This was essentially an isolated tragedy amid other more monumental human tragedies I was hearing about on the news in the 1990s. In particular I recall the events of the Balkans war unfolding on television, thinking how horrific it seemed. I completely failed to understand the events that were unfolding, and why there was a need for war at all. Dad told me that he vaguely remembered the Second World War, which was much worse than this. I remember not believing that anything could be much worse than the Balkans War I was seeing on television. This instilled a hatred of war, which has never left me into adulthood. Much smaller events of the 1990s opened other debates in my mind around the impact of personal character on one's career and general ability. It was impossible to escape seeing President Clinton being forced to stand down in 1998, thinking his political demise seemed unnecessary. I asked dad why what he did was so unforgivable, and that his personal life had nothing to do with his ability as a politician. He said that in his opinion, Clinton's main offence was that he lied to his nation. Had the American media known about the nature of the subsequent president, they might have reconsidered the vilification.

Although there were many events in the 1990s that one is happy to forget, there were many events that society obliged you to instil in the memory and keep there forever. The mantra was 'Remember this as you'll never see anything like this again in your lifetime'. There was a sense that everything was happening for the last time and that you had to cling onto everything before it passed you by like the view from a train's window. One example was seeing Hale Bop comet after a church event with mum and dad in 1997. We were at a Catholic celebration of the Passover and went outside afterwards as we were told the sky was clear enough to see the comet. I thought it resembled a mysterious smudged star; it had a lofty elegance but possibly was not worthy of the general hype. Another example was watching the solar eclipse in 1999. We sat in the garden and drank ginger beer while waiting for the eclipse to take place. We had a piece of cardboard with a hole in it at the ready, and saw that the sun had a slightly irregular shape for a few seconds. I remember observing the reactions of the birds in the garden who squawked frantically, clearly confused that the sky had taken on a purplish hue that was not quite like sunset. Another event that was massively hyped was the new Millennium. I was allowed into Norwich with my siblings, Gabby and Dan, to join in the millennium celebrations. It was expected that you had a specific activity planned for this event and we had decided to see what Norwich had in store. The people of Norwich were officially allowed to drink in the streets and by night it became a surreal place with people wandering around not really having anywhere to go. There was a sense of independence and excitement at being allowed out with the adults to wander the streets and listen to Abba's song 'Gimme Gimme Gimme a Man After Midnight' in front of Norwich town hall. But also I can remember the sense of anti-climax after midnight when the fireworks stopped and nothing had changed.

Catherine Pitt studied Biology, History, French and Art at A-level in Norwich. She became interested in the molecular world and decided to take her scientific career further. After studying a Science conversion course in Norwich, she left home to study Pharmacy at Manchester University from where she graduated with a first class degree. She currently lives in Newcastle and works as a clinical pharmacist at Sunderland Royal Hospital. Her favourite pastimes include reading, painting, watching films and socialising with her friends. She enjoys music and plays the trumpet in a band that she likes to think sounds like Dexy's Midnight Runners.

ACKNOWLEDGEMENTS

Firstly I wish to thank most sincerely those who contributed to the project; I am delighted with the quality of their work. Most of them fitted their writing into very busy lives and for that I am particularly grateful.

My special thanks to my daughter, Rebecca, who is not only a contributor, but has been enthusiastic and supportive throughout the project. Her constant advice and technical support have been invaluable. Thanks also to my daughter, Anna, who gave very sound advice about my introduction to this book. Pam Stanier agreed to check the proofs and made helpful comments which were much appreciated. My wife, Veronica, provided valuable advice at key moments in the development of the project for which I am most grateful.

I would also like to express my appreciation of Jimmy Wales and the fantastic web site, Wikipedia, which he created. I believe this is a wonderful resource without which I would not have been able to construct the 'Timeline of Social History'.

Finally, I must acknowledge the friendly team at Aspect Design. In particular I would like to thank Daniel Smith for his meticulous attention to detail – a quality I lack myself!

BIBLIOGRAPHY

BOOKS

Blom, Philipp *The Vertigo Years: Change and Culture in the West 1900–1914,* Weidenfeld and Nicolson (2008).

Terraine, John *The Mighty Continent: A View of Europe in the Twentieth Century,* British Broadcasting Corporation and Hutchinson (1974).

DOWNLOADS

Gillard D, *Education in England: a Brief History* (2011).
www.educationengland.org.uk/history/

Hicks J and Allen G, *A Century of Change: Trends in UK Statistics Since 1900,* Commons Library Research Paper 99/111 (1999).
www.parliament.uk/briefing-papers/RP99-111

UNICEF, *Child Poverty in Perspective: an Overview of Child Well-Being in Rich Countries,* Innocenti Report Card 7, Innocenti Research Centre (2007).
www.unicef-irc.org/publications/445

WEBSITES

Action for Smoking on Health: www.ash.org.uk *(Smoking)*

AVERT: www.avert.org/uk-statistics.htm *(HIV/Aids)*

BBC History:

   www.bbc.co.uk/ww2peopleswar/categories/c1162/
   (Childhood and Evacuation)

www.bbc.co.uk/history/british/Modern/windrush_01.shtml
(Windrush – the Passengers)

Cancer Research UK: www.cancerresearchuk.org *(Smoking)*

Guardian: www.guardian.co.uk/environment/2008/jan/10/nuclearpower.energy? *(Timeline: Nuclear Power in the United Kingdom)*

History Timelines: www.history-timelines.org.uk/events-timelines/07-computer-history-timeline.htm *(Computer History Timeline)*

NetValley: www.netvalley.com *(IT)*

Office of National Statistics: www.ons.gov.uk *(Road Casualties)*

Roll of Honour: www.roll-of-honour.com *(War Casualties)*

Spartacus Educational: www.spartacus.schoolnet.co.uk/Wbirth.htm *(Birth Control)*

TV History: www.tvhistory.btinternet.co.uk (History of TV)

Wikipedia: www.wikipedia.org

www.dinkytoys.ch *(Toys)*